DATE DUE

APR 27 1970

JUL 23 1970

OCT 12 1970

MAY 1972

THE CHRISTIAN SOCIETY

SERIES IN AMERICAN STUDIES

Editor-in-Chief: Joseph J. Kwiat
PROGRAM IN AMERICAN STUDIES
UNIVERSITY OF MINNESOTA

THE CHRISTIAN SOCIETY

By

GEORGE DAVIS HERRON

With a New Introduction by
MILTON CANTOR
DEPARTMENT OF HISTORY
UNIVERSITY OF MASSACHUSETTS

JOHNSON REPRINT CORPORATION

NEW YORK AND LONDON

1969

The edition reproduced here was originally
published in 1894.

Library of Congress
Catalog Card Number: 78-79659

Printed in the U. S. A.

INTRODUCTION

"In an age which mammon rules," George Herron declared, "when property is protected at the expense of humanity, when the state regards material things as more sacred than human beings, the gospel of the kingdom of God . . . needs to be terribly preached as the judgment of love to the brutal cynicism of the market, to the industrial despotisms. . . ." Herron's reaction to social and economic conditions is representative of a small, highly articulate group of radical Christian clergymen; and I use the word "representative," of course, to indicate the paradigmatic, not the average. This reaction must be seen against the background of industrial conflict and the alleged unethical practices of the business community, which were major concerns of social Christianity generally and which were part of the seamless web of post-Civil War history.

The postwar industrial revolution made it impossible for people to lead the life Christ intended; or so it seemed to some Protestant clergymen. But the clerical majority insouciantly disregarded the changed economic circumstances of American life, and the attendant social misery and parlous conditions. Rather this majority invoked the ethical code fashioned for an older agrarian, preindustrial order. It emphasized economic individualism, tended to endorse the business-oriented society and to apologize for business practices. It openly supported the Gospel of Wealth, finding justification for acquisitive and entrepreneurial impulses, and it remained smugly preoccupied with the individual's salvation. Consequently, this majority limited its reforms to correcting individual vices—such as intemperance, dancing, profanity, Sabbath-breaking. Such a pietistic and doctrinally conservative program, with its conventional stress upon spiritual regeneration, effectively insulated most Protestant clergymen against a program of social ethics and social amelioration until the late nineties. Even the Baptist and Methodist clergy, who once ministered to the poor, now often displayed concern only for the affluent. Indeed, all Protestant denominations neglected the unchurched masses of urban America and were indifferent to and on occasion hostile to the cause of labor.

But not all clergymen and denominations remained aloof from the social and economic currents swirling around them. The changes, after all, were momentous, dramatic, and far-reaching. There were great increases in manufacturing, the accumulation of vast new wealth, the concentration and combination of industry ("the centralization of wealth," Herron pejoratively described it), the emergence of the corporation and of its offspring —the trust, the great influx of immigrants and rural dispossessed into urban centers, the expanding railroads and, concomitantly, the commercialization of agriculture. These developments transformed American society. Satirized by Mark Twain as the "Gilded Age," this new society—shaped in the twin crucibles of Civil War and Pittsburgh iron furnaces—rejected the old ethical proprieties and produced sprawling cities. Their slums were rife with crime and immorality, claimed rural America, and seemed to threaten the unraveling of the social fabric.

Such conditions evoked a compulsive concern about society by an energetic minority of Protestant clergymen, and prompted a new surge of criticism that increasingly concentrated upon the new and staggering social problems—of urban sanitation and disease, misgovernment and poverty, industrial warfare, and the rapid growth of socialism. Henry George's scheme for socialization of land rents also influenced these few alert ministers, and they read *Progress and Poverty* as a breviary. Perhaps the pre-Civil War revivals provided an instructive tradition to draw upon. Most assuredly, the liberalizing and fundamentally ethical force of Unitarianism was a mordant factor since it traditionally recognized, more than any other Protestant denomination, the church's obligation to society and sought to socialize Christian doctrine. Nor should Populism be neglected since a number of social gospel leaders, Herron included, were Midwestern in origins and profoundly influenced by frontier conditions; further, they clearly identified with rural grievances, agrarian unrest, and Populist antagonism to monopoly and "plutocracy"—the values which shaped their boyhood. Finally, there was the external stimulus provided by English Christian socialism; and the writings of Charles Kingsley and Frederick Maurice influenced some social gospel ministers. Social Christianity, in sum, was the natural offspring of economic conditions, external forces, and an indigenous cultural-religious heritage; indeed, it expressed a criticism of conventional religious and political thought that was as old as the Gospel and the high moral aspiration of Judaic prophecy.

The "Religion of Humanity" nonetheless was advanced by only a small minority of Protestant ministers, and Winthrop Hudson correctly refers to Walter Rauschenbusch as a "lonely prophet." Rauschenbusch himself recalled the movement in the 1890's as "a time of lonesomeness"; and, he continued, "we were few, and we shouted in the wilderness." Certainly, the ministry's rank-and-file held fast to the old orthodoxies, content to voice clerical commonplaces about self-help, and to conceive of social amelioration in terms of organized charities. Only a few found something unlovely and unchristian about the Gilded Age. This minority in the late 1880's began to evolve toward what became known as the "new theology." They were spurred on by the emergence of monopolies, the accumulation of vast new wealth, the plight of the urban poor, the social impotence of the clergy as a whole, and most urgently the need to check the growing antagonism of labor when confronted by hard evidence of business-church collusion.

Labor's militancy and solidarity, as well as its progressive alienation from the church, alarmed the more sensitive Protestant clergymen. The postwar decline of real wages which forced children into premature labor in the factories and contributed to the seething labor violence of the 1870's, the nation-wide strikes of the mid-eighties, the Homestead and Pullman walkouts of the early nineties, and the reaction to blacklists and lockouts which employers practiced, inspired and prefigured bloody social conflict. These events galvanized a spirited clerical minority into socially-oriented activities.

Those who embraced the social gospel were divided on a number of issues, most obviously on the question of socialism, though in varying degree they all rejected laissez-faire and favored government control over utilities, railroads, *inter alia;* and they all urged, again with variations, both socialized Christianity and Christianized society, that is, they sought to socialize Christian thought and practices. Unanimously alarmed over the social disorganization of American life, they responded in a number of ways, usually by founding settlement houses, an idea borrowed from Toynbee Hall, or by devising organizations that would deal with particular evils—such as the plight of working mothers or intemperance.

Sharing a common concern, all votaries of the social gospel contributed to a literature of social commitment, helped to found theological schools, worked to introduce courses in sociology and social work in the curriculum of seminaries and universities, and appeared before groups that discussed problems of labor and capital. But beyond this collective pattern of activity the moderates refused to go. A more radical bloc, the Christian socialists, went much further, impelled as they were by empty pews in slum churches, the misuse of great wealth, and the unspeakable misery that was apparent everywhere. Not limiting themselves to pleas for a new social spirit or a few reforms like day nurseries, they rejected the existing social and economic order. They spoke in terms of crisis and employed the rhetoric of class warfare. More often than not, they regarded the conflict of labor and capital as at the vital center of the social problem. But they also expressed anxiety over ancillary matters, such as conditions of urban life or the discontent of a sullen working class. The gravamen of their charge, however, centered on unrestricted economic individualism—that is, upon the philosophical assumptions of American capitalism—and they launched a direct frontal assault on classical economic doctrine. In so doing, to be sure, they ran athwart the long Protestant tradition which celebrated self-reliance and hard work, and which sanctified unrestrained individual effort. But they could respond by invoking an equally hallowed ethic of secular benevolence—

the historic Christian recognition of the spiritual worth of the single human being, and the need to do everything possible to prevent his denigration.

That a growing number of clergymen were converted to the cause of Christian socialism was a reflection upon the harsh depression years, 1893–1895. Their number remained small, but they brought the radical social gospel to maturity by 1895. Among them, and the dominant figure in the early 1890's, was George Davis Herron (1862–1925). Born in Indiana, the son of lower-class, devoutly religious parents of Scottish origins, Herron was forced into apprenticeship in a print shop.

Herron's association with the Congregational Church began at thirteen. Four years later, a "divine illumination" directed him to college—in preparation for what he believed to be a religious mission—and "the dark pale, brown-eyed Indianian" enrolled at Ripon College in Wisconsin in 1879. Relying upon his early print-shop training, Herron edited the college paper as a means of financing his education, but the poor health and inadequate funds that troubled his early years eventually forced him to leave school. After moving to Minnesota he worked in another print shop and dreamed of a literary career. But he was destined

for a different vocation. Still possessed of a
divinely-ordained sense of mission, he decided to
enter the ministry in 1883. Herron's first ministry
was in a newly organized congregation in Zanes-
ville, Ohio; and from there, in 1887, he went to a
larger and older church in Lake Mills, Wisconsin.
Two years later he was called to the pulpit of the
Lake City, Minnesota, parish. And he was installed
as associate pastor of the Burlington, Iowa, Congregational Church in December 1891.

In the manner of all Western revivalists, Herron sought to awaken his listeners to a personal
and visible repentence, to produce a conviction of
sin and of eternal punishment for those who would
not accept the proffered hand of God and thereby
come to an "experience" of divine love and grace.
True to the sources of evangelical faith, Herron's
religion derived from a feeling of direct personal
access to God rather than from elaborate doctrinal
statements. "While I find myself in accord with
the evangelical theology of the day . . . ," he
affirmed, "my belief in God and my thought concerning Him have not been formed by either the
theology of the creeds or the philosophy of the
schools."

Herron, in the fashion of revivalists, was a

preacher, not a theologian; he was a popularizer and a prophet. Fired by a personal intimation of God and goaded by his sense of mission, Herron embraced a religion that gave him a strong emotional charge. It came out of an inner conviction that God was with him. "I have never been without the inner consciousness of God's compelling and restraining presence," he declared, and continued: "I cannot remember when the Eternal Word was ever silent in my soul." He recalled how his mother

> asked God to give her a child who should be His servant. She received me as from God and gave me back to God as her freewill offering. She besought God to keep me upon the altar of a perfect sacrifice in the service of His Christ and her Redeemer. She told God of her willingness to have me drink of Christ's cup and be baptized with his baptism, if needful for my entire consecration to His purpose in my life . . . . nothing has ever been able to separate her from the belief that in bringing me into the world she had fulfilled the purpose of her being, and she never doubted that I would be a messenger of God to my fellow-men.

Nor for that matter did Herron himself. Such

recollections shaped a messianic obsession typical of revivalistic preachers. Moreover, he believed in a conscious conversion that placed "experience" over "profession." His own "experience" was characteristic of immediate crisis conversion.

I saw the selfishness, the pride, the falseness, the absolute unholiness of my heart [Herron confessed] until I could bear the revelation no more . . . . I groped in that horror of darkness which settles down upon a soul when it knows that there is no sound thing in it, and that it merits nothing but eternal death and endless night . . . . I knew that nowhere had I an inch of standing ground save the mercy of God . . . . Jonathan Edward's Enfield sermon was, at that time, the only thing real enough to answer to my experience. But out of this horrible pit I cried unto the Lord and he heard me, lifting me up and planting my feet upon the rock of his salvation. When neither body nor brain could longer endure the divine testing and searching of soul, God revealed to me his Christ, and I knew what it meant to be saved. I was now not only a child of God by birth and calling, but a redeemed child, bought by the blood of Christ, cleansed by the sufferings of God.

Small wonder that memory of these events produced a personal, intuitive, emotional religion; or that Herron would preach the importance of individual conversion and interpret social injustice in terms which reflected his schooling in Western evangelism. Such rhetoric as "social sin" and the "redemption of society" suggested the relation of social reform with the categories of Christian experience. Indeed, Herron's approach to the social gospel can be best understood in terms of seeking to correct an irrelevant clerical piety and to connect Christian belief with the search for social justice.

Herron's formative years, therefore, were devoted to pursuing two lines—one socio-economic and the other theological. He knew rural poverty and understood Populist unrest. But there were other influences. Witness, for example, Henry George, who proclaimed the immensely attractive message of brotherhood and gradualism. Herron at one time even advocated the single-tax panacea, believing it would provide the "elemental basis for the ideal society." Nor was George alone. Mazzini —"my best beloved Master, next to Jesus"—also made a strong impact. He was influenced, too, by the English social reformer John Ruskin and apparently by Savonarola, Calvin, Leo Tolstoi,

George Bancroft, and, unusual among Christian socialists, Georg Hegel. Herron, upon a superficial reading of Hegel, endorsed his belief in the unity of ideal and real and, by extension, the unity of the divine and the human, doing so with a passion which Emerson in his most transcendental moments would have envied.

Christ, to Herron, was no afterthought, but the ideal with which God started out. He was what Adam failed to be. He was the way in which God identified Himself with humanity. God was not ignored; and Herron's was the suffering God—a loving, forgiving, merciful God at work on earth. But Herron's God was best known through Christ. Jesus was an empty vessel, and God poured into Him all of His own incarnation. By so doing, God became one with humanity.

This ontological view governing the image of man is unique, shared by none of Herron's contemporaries in precisely this way and one must turn back to the Transcendental faith in man's divinity to approximate it. Not that emphasis on Christ was unknown to Christian socialists. They all sought to bring Jesus' teachings to bear on current social issues—in the hope that the social order might be Christianized and the Kingdom of God realized on earth. But Herron, the central figure in the Kingdom movement, embraced it in extreme and exclusive form. He is both prolix and confused in his exposition, but man clearly is the recipient of God's grace and by it he becomes a divine incarnation.

Faith is the only guide to salvation since, true to the Calvinism that shaped him, Herron finds that man cannot deliver himself. Indeed, he affirms man's sense of sinfulness and his absolute dependence upon God's sovereign mercy as the only road to grace. Still Herron's theology is not Antinominian in its implications: crisis conversion assumes that deliverance from evil is a response of will and that, however it clashes with predestinarian Calvinism, God could only work in this way. Consonant with the self-conscious faith in man exhibited in Western revivalism, Herron can claim that God's redemption needed man's assistance. God is praying to men to deliver Him from evil in the world.

Flatly denying any dualism, Herron insists that the humanity and divinity of Jesus were essentially the same. Thus Jesus for him prefigures the divine humanity which is to come. Such a view is inextricably enmeshed with his belief in the redemption of society through the sacrifices of the individual, a proposition that is wholly at odds with the Gospel of Wealth. Words like "redemption" and "self-sacrifice" are sprinkled throughout the selections in *The Christian Society;* and the image of Christ on the Cross has great metaphorical value. No Christian is true to it or "true to his Christ . . . who is not a vicarious sufferer for his fellow-men." Man's goal must be to emulate Christ's example, rather than seek earthly possessions. The man of wealth was singled out; he must be "a little Christ in the world," or else he has "made a disastrous and irreparable business failure."

Herron's "Christian society" would arrive when man followed Christ's law of love, when man surrendered to God's Christ and, like Christ, sacrificed himself to his fellowmen. By this act, which contributed to the redemption of society, man would fully open his life to God and achieve his own salvation. Blurring the distinction between spiritual and material worlds, Herron affirmed that man's life must be Christlike—the way of the cross—and the end product of living like Christ would be a Christianizing of society itself. This spacious and vague idea of redemption by sacrifice was, for Herron, divinely granted to man. Sacrifice was the true test of faith for the disciple of Christ, and commitment measured by it; and Herron, more than anyone else in his day, centered his religion in the cross and in the doctrine of sacrifice.

Driven by his grand mission, Herron never adequately outlined his "Christian society" on earth, though it provides the main thrust of his early sermons and his first books—*The Larger Christ* (1891) and *The New Redemption* (1893). There is no detail about such a society and no apparent effort to reconcile the means-end dichotomy. Nor is there anything concrete about the nature of industrial democracy or about the future socialist state. In this same vague sense, and like all converts to Christian socialism, he declares war *à outrance* against competition and places himself in opposition to a long and powerful Protestant tradition encouraging industry and self-reliance. Herbert Spencer and William Graham Sumner, the chief spokesmen for economic individualism, are singled out for a withering indictment: their principles amounted to "the assertion of self against God and humanity."

Herron would eventually turn toward socialism.

He would find private property to be sinful, urge state control of railroads and utilities, endorse Marx's view of a class society and class struggle, and find Christianity and socialism synonymous. Here, too, however, he was irritatingly general. He never advanced any hard suggestions about the new world order or how it might be realized. He only claimed that the faith of Christ's disciples would usher in this new order—the kingdom on earth.

In harmony with every Christian socialist, Herron sought a new social role for the church. But more than most, he condemned religious institutions. His religion, we have noted, was personal and charismatic rather than institutional. He had no need for liturgical expression or for any intellectual foundation for religious instruction. But it was not merely a matter of priorities. In an age when belief and worship had become externalized as never before and when the problem of human welfare seemed to be ignored, Herron was vigorously anti-church. Jesus and his principles were inevitably contrasted to institutional forms. "The Spirit of Christ," Herron declared, "is coming to anoint the factory, the mine, the railroad, to preach good tidings to the poor, and set at liberty them that are bruised." Jesus, he continued, "did not believe in religious institutions and their teachers, because they were seeking to draw all men unto themselves instead of unto God his Father and the Father of the people."

A pietistic perfectionist, Herron's outlook was that of a premillenialist: Christ would return to earth before the millenium and set up on earth a kingdom under his personal rule. The vision of resurrection accompanied this prospect. A "messianic age" would come, Herron predicted, "educated in the science of redemption to bear away the sins of society and bring in the thousand years of peace." Such a vision always sought a perfect moral freedom, as distinct from that of a clerical majority which sought merely social and moral order. It also sought a return to the pure, apostolic, primitive church. It assumed that religion demanded more than simply getting oneself in harmony with the moral law, that it meant translating that law into action.

Herron was in many ways a representative Christian socialist. Certainly he was typical in his insistent belief that capitalist culture was sinful, that it produced evil, that it flouted the laws of God. From his earliest writings, such as *The New*

Redemption, there was a continual sniping at affluence, especially because it denied labor an equable share in the social benefits of American life. Herron, more than most, exalted the work of the ordinary worker, employing rhetoric reminiscent of Luther and Calvin: "He who would interpret God, and know what God's work is, will not find him away from the common toils and places of men, but in the midst of people . . . . The poorest man who works for his bread may wear the crown of a divine kingship." Finally, Herron also is representative in his desire to formulate rules of conduct rather than theological statements. "Religion," he declared, "is not something besides life, not a withdrawal of life from fellowships, but the pouring out of life as a sacrifice to God in the service of man." ✔

And yet Herron was unique, almost a social outcast among Protestants generally. For his views—on such institutions as marriage and education—were too unorthodox to be acceptable to most Protestants. Perhaps this was the reason for Herron's failure to make a major impact on American Protestantism. Or perhaps Herron failed because he was too much the individualist to pay the price of organizational approbation.

Herron, to be sure, did not lack for popularity. Understandably, the "Western messiah" had regional appeal. His attacks on monopoly and social inequities, advanced in language that throbbed with religious intensity, endeared him to many who were possessed by the same demonology. Conversely, he was swept along with Populism for a time and had high hopes for it: "The new social movement springing out of the soil of the Western States," declared the *Kingdom* (Herron's periodical), "is assuming a Socialistic aspect . . . . I look to see out of the Western States the greatest religious movement since the reformation. It will be a revival of faith closely akin to Primitive Christianity."

This is not to say that Herron lacked for popularity among urban radicals; he found supporters and sympathizers everywhere, owing to the economic discontent produced by the depression in the United States and to the work of other pioneer Social Gospel spokesmen. Herron's work formed a clearly marked pattern before the 1880's had run their course, but it was on September 22, 1890, with his address before the Minnesota Congregational Club, "The Message of Jesus to Men of Wealth" (written, Herron recalled, as if "the personal

Jesus were standing over his study table . . . , saying unto him, 'Write thus, and thus, and thus' "), that Herron became nationally known. Thereafter, his great oratorical abilities and charismatic powers inevitably attracted attention—for his sermons were full of vivid imagery and charged with emotion. He had a message for the heart, a call to return to the pristine faith of the church and of the fathers; and he framed it in simple Calvinist terms of eternal struggle between good and evil, terms that appealed to simple constituencies everywhere. By the mid-nineties, then, he was certainly a nationally known Christian radical. Though occasionally avoided by respectable congregations, he was popularized by men like Josiah Strong, W. D. P. Bliss, and Benjamin O. Flower. Herron became the prophet of a new religious movement—one pietistic and mystical in its thrust—and eventually he lost touch with the churches and embraced socialism.

Herron was the first American preacher to combine the revivalist methods of Moody and Ira Sankey with the aspirations of Christian radicalism. His Kingdom movement was both socio-ethical and theological in character. It arose out of the need to deal honorably with human and social needs, but it was primarily religious in emphasis, which is understandable since Herron was by instinct and temperament a social revivalist rather than a socialist. His views were governed by emotion, we have observed, rather than by reasoned conclusion. His vision lacked system, for it was nonstructured, rhetorical, elusive, and mystical. As a result, he was increasingly isolated from creative contact with other social gospel leaders, uncommitted to any viewpoint other than his own, inflexibly certain of the rightness of his ideal, rejecting pragmatic acquiescence in favor of the intrinsic worth of his principles. Consequently, he was sealed off from the accommodations essential to successful social progress and from the explosive possibilities inherent in the moderate social gospel.

Herron, however, was both representative and anomalous. He made more than an isolated and ritualistic gesture of dissent from American capitalism; he was the prophet of a new humanism, a new concept of progress that attracted wide support. He simplified ideas, established a claim to truth and, in the union of both, demanded a commitment to action. And those who listened to his *cri de coeur* against capitalist society were transformed. Herron himself merits the emphasis lavished upon him. There are some writers, said Jean Giraudoux, whose lives are more important to us than their works. He did not have Herron in mind, but Herron illustrates perfectly the idea he goes on to develop—that there are writers whose lives and whose works run together, so that it is the man we read in his writings. However repetitious, hortatory, and sentimental, the selections in *The Christian Society* are the mirror of the man and his turbulent times.

Milton Cantor

SELECTED BIBLIOGRAPHY

Abell, Aaron I. *The Urban Impact of American Protestantism, 1865–1900*. Hamden, Connecticut, 1962.

Destler, Chester. *American Radicalism, 1865–1901*. New London, Connecticut, 1964.

Dombrowski, James. *The Early Days of Christian Socialism in America*. New York, 1936.

Gabriel, Ralph H. *The Course of American Democratic Thought*. New York, 1940.

Handy, Robert. "George Herron and the Kingdom Movement," *Church History* XIX (1950), 97–115.

———. "George D. Herron and the Social Gospel in American Protestantism, 1890–1901," Univ. of Chicago Ph.D. dissertation, 1949.

Herron, George D. *The Call of the Cross*. New York, 1892.

———. *The Christian State*. New York, 1895.

———. *The Larger Christ*. New York, 1893.

———. *The New Redemption*. New York, 1893.

———. *A Plea for the Gospel*. New York, 1892.

Hopkins, Charles. *The Rise of the Social Gospel*

in American Protestantism, 1865–1915. New Haven, Connecticut, 1940.

Hudson, Winthrop. *American Protestantism.* Chicago, Illinois, 1961.

————. *The Great Tradition of the American Churches.* New York, 1953.

————. *Religion in America.* New York, 1965.

May, Henry. *Protestant Churches and Industrial America.* New York, 1963.

Olmstead, Clifton. *Religion in America, Past and Present.* Englewood Cliffs, New Jersey, 1961.

Schlesinger, Arthur M. "A Critical Period in American Religion, 1875–1900," Massachusetts Historical Society, *Proceedings,* LXIV (1932), 523–547.

Smith, H. Sheldon, *et al. American Christianity: An Historical Interpretation with Representative Documents.* 2 vols. New York, 1960.

THE CHRISTIAN SOCIETY.

THE CHRISTIAN SOCIETY

BY

GEORGE D. HERRON, D. D.

The E. D. Rand Professor of Applied Christianity in Iowa College. Author of
" The Larger Christ," " The New Redemption," etc.

"Are we advancing toward anarchy or toward a new mode of things,—toward
dissolution or toward a transformed life? All ask themselves this question;
all could resolve it, if the point of view of each man were not narrowed by his
position in some one of the adverse camps."—*Joseph Mazzini.*

FLEMING H. REVELL COMPANY
CHICAGO   NEW YORK   TORONTO
1894

I Dedicate this Book

to

President George A. Gates, D. D.,

My Fellow-worker

in the Kingdom of God.

PREFACE.

EXCEPTING the fourth, the following chapters were prepared and spoken, in February, as a course of lectures to the students of Michigan University, Ann Arbor, under the auspices of the Students' Christian Association and the two Bible Chairs recently established in connection with the University. They have just been repeated, at the request of theological students and pastors, at Princeton, New Jersey. They have also been given, in whole or in part, to the students of Indiana State University, Bloomington; of Lawrence University, Appleton, Wisconsin; of Union Theological Seminary, New York City; and the first has recently been given as an address to the Congregational Club of Brooklyn, New York. They are now given to the people in this form. The fourth chapter was spoken to the Congregational Club of Minnesota in September, 1891. It has since gone through different

forms and editions of publication, and is now
included in this volume, that it may be more
permanently preserved.

I wish to say, in publishing these lectures,
that no institution, no organization, no particular school of thought or fellowship of men,
is in any wise responsible for the beliefs and
convictions — I have no opinions — I herein
express.   For these expressions I alone should
be held accountable to the people, as I shall
be to God.

I have not spoken, as some would say, to
discredit, but rather to glorify the church.   I
would save the church from the false position
of existing and working for its own glory and
religious aggrandizement, from the fatal Jewish position of seeking to bring the world under
the dominion of itself, and speak some word
that would help to convert it to the Christian
pursuit of sacrificing itself for the world.   I
would have the church become the incarnation
and representative of Jesus in bearing away
the sins of society ; in being rejected by the
proud and selfish and mighty, that it may
bring deliverance to the captives of social tyr-

annies, and preach the gospel of the kingdom
of God to the people. I would see the church
glorified with the glory that Jesus had upon
the cross, and sanctified with the disposition
which made him of no reputation in his own
eyes.

The church was not sent to be an institutional dominion, but a sacrificial and redemptive life in the world. Yet the church is not
engaged in sacrifice and redemption, so much
as in artificial organization ; not engaged in
discerning and teaching right from wrong, so
much as in definition of doctrines. The anal-
ogy between Protestant Christendom in relation to its mission of social redemption, and
the relation of the Jewish church to the first
appearance of the Son of God,. is true. I am
haunted continually with the vision of the living Jesus weeping over our majestic temples of
worship, our halls of theology, our conven-
tions of religion, as though he were again in
the sacred sorrow of that weeping over Jerusalem, his heart again broken because only the
remnant may receive the mission which the
institution rejects.

The coming social incarnation of the Son of God is the church's present day of visitation. Will the church know its visitation or put the Christ of judgment to a social crucifixion ?

GEORGE D. HERRON.

Iowa College, Grinnell, Iowa,
        March 5, 1894.

CONTENTS.

PAGE

I. THE SCIENTIFIC GROUND OF A CHRISTIAN
    SOCIOLOGY 15

II. THE CHRISTIAN CONSTITUTION OF SOCIETY 51

III. THE GOSPEL OF JESUS TO THE POOR . . 73

IV. THE MESSAGE OF JESUS TO MEN OF WEALTH 99

V. THE POLITICAL ECONOMY OF THE LORD'S
    PRAYER 125

CONTENTS

I. ....

II. ....

III. ....

IV. ....

V. ....

I.

THE SCIENTIFIC GROUND OF A

CHRISTIAN SOCIOLOGY.

"But, whatever be the form in which they are destined to be shaped, the work which the Christian societies, as societies, have to do, in the days that are to come, is not inferior to any work which has lain before them at any epoch of their history. For the air is charged with thunder, and the times that are coming may be times of storm. There are phenomena beneath the surface of society of which it would be hardly possible to overrate the significance. There is a widening separation of class from class : there is a growing social strain : there is a disturbance of the political equilibrium : there is the rise of an educated proletariat. To the problems which these phenomena suggest Christianity has the key. Its unaccomplished mission is to reconstruct society on the basis of brotherhood. What it has to do it does, and will do, in and through organization. At once profoundly individual and profoundly socialistic, its tendency to association is not so much an incident of its history as an essential element of its character. It spiritualizes that ineradicable instinct which draws man to man and makes society not a convention but a necessity. But the framing of its organization is left to human hands. To you and me and men like ourselves is committed, in these anxious days, that which is at once an awful responsibility and a splendid destiny — to transform this modern world into a Christian society, to change the socialism which is based on the assumption of clashing interests into the socialism which is based on the sense of spiritual union, and to gather together the scattered forces of a divided Christendom into a confederation in which organization will be of less account than fellowship with one Spirit and faith in one Lord — into a communion wide as human life and deep as human need — into a Church which shall outshine even the golden glory of its dawn by the splendor of its eternal noon."
— *Edwin Hatch.*

THE SCIENTIFIC GROUND OF A
CHRISTIAN SOCIOLOGY.

THE social strain of this winter of 1893 and 1894 is the beginning of the first real test of the worth of our American civilization, which must be known by its fruits. Whether swiftly or slowly, the strain will intensify until it proves to be either the formative or consuming trial of our government. It may seem unwise and revolutionary to so prophesy. But danger comes to a people through warnings unheeded rather than warnings spoken. Revolution is caused by seeking to substitute expediency for justice ; by trying to make the past the security oi the present. The historian of the future, looking back on our present crisis, will judge us with a severity that our stupid national conceit, that the wicked moral blindness of our industrialism, cannot now understand. This social strain, this winter of unemployment and want, is without excuse to a right-

eous reason. There is no war; no pestilence;
no failure of harvests. There is an abundance
in our land for the people. Yet this richest
nation of the world, in the midst of a material
prosperity so marvelous as to become the object of political worship, suddenly finds a vast
population face to face with famine, depend-
ent upon some quality of public philanthropy.
After all I have seen and heard, I believe the
terrible facts of our social situation have been
mainly suppressed, and but meagerly revealed
by the public press.

The causes of this situation, of this wide
and fearful impoverishment, are profounder
than any which the press has discussed. This
is but incidentally a monetary crisis. Its
cause and cure lie not in silver and tariff; in
the change of political parties. It is the direct result of the centralization of wealth, of
the investment of the control of industry, in
the hands of the cunning and strong, who in-
directly rule the lives and economies of the
people, with no responsibility for their welfare; with entire unaccountability to their will.
This crisis is a divine warning against the irresponsible egoism produced by a false science

of society. The development of this egoism is industrial despotism, the thrones and chains of which, though invisible, are yet the wickedest and bitterest the people have ever endured. This false science has given us the hardest masters and the most helpless slavery. Whether we condemn or hold guiltless the largest gainers of wealth and authority by our false economy of production and distribution, whether we regard them as victims or makers of this economy, the social strain is a call to the clearest minds, the purest energies, the divinest passions for humanity, to be immediate and intent upon the discovery and revelation of a true science of society. For the government of the future will be industrial, and statesmanship will be sociological.

Sociology has not yet become a science. It has bewildered our social troubles with an anarchy of figures, but has found no ground for human relations; it has given us no constructive knowledge of social order. The observance of existing phenomena apart from moral facts and forces, a reverence for statistics and an aversion to principles, has been the fatuity of all attempts to create a science of sociology.

2

No sociological method is so wholly unscientific, or so misses the chief facts, as that which confines itself to observing and tabulating social conditions. Figures lie above all other media of human expression. Many will listen with interest to facts which are seen, quite as ready to believe erroneous statistics as true, where one will hear and obey a right principle. Unless it be primarily a science of righteousness, sociology cannot be a science of society. Its work only begins with the observance of existing phenomena. It must give society a knowledge of how to create phenomena that shall be just. When it attempts to be scientific through the inductive study of social conditions and statistics, without making the moral causes of wrong conditions the main object of study and correction, it passes into that profound ignorance that always darkens the understanding that has no ethical vision. Sociology can become a science only by becoming a science of redemption. By grounding society in right social faiths and laying the axe of truth at the roots of social falsehoods, by regenerating society with right social motives and leading it with right social

visions, will sociology fulfill its scientific vocation, which is the education of society in
justice.

Sociology must be a science of justice to be
a science of society. Until it become a fellowship of justice, society is not a reality; it is
still the divine phantom which has drawn out
the history of man, the phantom which the
holiest efforts of the race have pursued only to
be beaten back by the forces of the long night
in which tyranny reigns over ignorance and
weakness. Sociology has not been, nor has it
thought of being, a science of just relations.
The various social sciences are directed toward
charities, which have served society nobly and
well, but which hardly touch the heart of the
social question. The true sociology will discover and interpret the justice which will leave
little occasion for what we now understand by
charity and philanthropy. These are terms
which have lost their moral intent and force.
Men enriched by making society their prey
may graciously administer organizations for
the relief of the poor. Fortunes amassed under legal forms by cruelest oppression and
extortion, by cunning that knows neither con-

science nor shame, by speculation that regards
no social suffering or injury, may enable men
to stand at the head of great philanthropies
and endow public institutions.   In their last
analysis, philanthropy and charity are justice.
Where there is no passion for justice there is
no brother love.   Unless we will and work
that they have social justice, we have neither
charity nor philanthropy toward men.   If we
are scientifically charitable, we shall not excuse the wealth produced by social wrong with
a display of interest in some form of charity,
or an educational endowment, but demand
that its possessors cease to prey upon social
needs ; that they cease to make ignorance and
weakness their power and riches.   The philanthropy that is a science, the brother love
that is wise and bold to discern justice, will
discover and apply the principles that are
authoritative to deny the right of men to rob
and slay by the indirection of economic custom ; to deny the right of the strong to put
their burdens on the weak, and the right of
wealth to social irresponsibility.   A scientific
method of social correction will bear its mightiest corrective forces upon those who through

legerdemain or inheritance have acquired the means to live in luxury and idleness ; in the dilettanteisms of culture and fashionable benevolence. Theirs is the real pauperism which victimizes society — a pauperism immeasurably more immoral and disgusting than that of the tramp or beggar who furnishes us opportunity for science and suffering, and too often for wicked amusement. The parasitism which costs, which is consuming the life and hope of the social organism, and which charity and philanthropy must first of all bring to judgment, sits upon thrones of commerce and industry, and dwells in palaces, and founds great philanthropies. Unless charity and philanthropy be the pursuit of justice, they are neither scientific nor ethical, however exact their knowledge of conditions, or noble their purpose to help. Sociology must give the various social sciences a foundation and vision of justice, or the hypocrisy of social tyranny will make them the opportunity to conceal the real social question, and delay judgment and true correction, until divine evolution shall proceed through retributive revolution.

The field of sociological science must be the

faiths that form character and inspire activity. The first sociological fact is that human relations depend upon what people believe. Society is a living organism rather than a structural organization, having its roots in the common faith. It is in faith that political institutions have their foundation and growth. Production and distribution have been according to the principles inspiring men's motives and ruling their actions. Commerce, government, and civilization historically follow the path of those who seek righteousness. The chief economic factor of Europe in the twelfth century was the conscience of Bernard of Clairvaux. The commercial and political supremacy of the Anglo-Saxon peoples is largely due to the faith of Calvin and Cromwell in the divine government of the world. What nature is in its relation to society, how it acts and what fruits it yields, depend upon what man is. Instead of climate making the man, as Taine and Spencer would have us assume, it would be quite as true to say that man makes the climate. Moral degradation violates nature and desolates the face of the earth, while moral purpose makes the rocks and sands fruitful. It is not a prophetic rhapsody, but natural law, that perfect righteousness would cause the desert to literally blossom as a rose, and make the earth a garden of the Lord.

That sociology must have a ground of faith is not an assumption; it is not even a question. Nothing is falser than that faith has nothing to do with science. All science is the discovery of faith. This is even truer of physical than of theological science; for theology often builds upon the ground of pure assumption, or prejudice, having in it no quality of faith, while natural science has believed in the growth of knowledge. Whether sociology will or no, it cannot help starting with some quality of faith in regard to man, his environment and destiny. There is a question only as to what that faith shall be.

Jesus Christ offers sociology the only scientific ground of discovering all the facts and forces of life. That ground is his revelation of universal unity. However unique we regard the person of Jesus, however difficult we regard the interpretation of his teachings, however imperfect their literary transmission to us, it is clear that the vision which so flooded the soul of this teacher, which makes his person the light of the world, was the oneness in substance and elements and forces, of the universe. The conception of a universe of separative elements, of fragments and dualisms, was to Jesus the horrible blasphemy that had darkened the understandings of men. Dualism was devilism; it was the very essence of evil; it was itself the gross darkness that had hidden God from men, disfellowshiped them from each other, causing all their wars and lusts and anarchies, causing them to sit solitary in the misery and desolation of selfishness, enslaved and crushed under its tyranny. That which sociology needs in order to be a progressive science of society, in order to learn and teach a constructive knowledge of human relations, is the ground of universal unity upon which Jesus stood. Until it becomes a science of this unity it cannot be a science of society, and society will remain the baffled effort of history. Society must be unity with all that is, with God and man, with the moral and the physical, with the known and the unknown, or it cannot be society in fact. The

realization of society will be the realization of
the universal unity in human relations. The
just society, the society that perfectly appre-
hends the resources and directs the forces
of nature, will be the unity of the life of
the people with the life of God. For, if
there be any sense in the universe, if there
be a universe, the nature of man, the nature
of nature, and the nature of God are one.
And, according to Jesus, the one, the all, the
universe is Christian.

I use the term Christian to define a sacrificial and redemptive quality of life or action;
of fact or force. Jesus became the Christ
through the offering of his whole life to God
upon the altar of his love for man. His
Christhood was his power and will to sacrifice.
His eternal sonship was the perfect realization
of an eternal quality of life in human relations.
All the forces of the universe, so he revealed,
are sacrificial and redemptive. Eternal life is
the eternal sacrifice of life. Christianity is the
realization of the universal sacrifice, of the
philanthropy of God, of the redemptive righteousness of Christ, in society. It is more
than religion, conduct, or duty; more than

worship, creed, or habit ; more than opinion, custom, or church.   The fulfillment of Christianity will be the mutual sacrifice of God and his world in the society of a common need; the perfect obedience of man to the law of love revealed in the sacrifice of Christ, and spoken of by him as a new commandment which was to distinguish his disciples; which was to define his society, among the religions and economies of the world.   The method of sacrifice, by which this law executes itself, marks its eternal quality and universal force ; it is this that makes it Christian.   It is not the ancient Hebrew law that man shall love his neighbor as himself.   He who loves his neighbor no more than himself has not taken the first step in Christian discipleship. A man may keep all the Ten Commandments, including the Hebrew law of love, and turn sorrowfully away when perceiving the heart of law in the sacrifice of love.   The man who loves his neighbor no more than himself has made no sacrifice ; he has organized his life on the Hebrew, the conservative, but not on the Christian or redemptive basis.   The new commandment which Jesus gave, which we do not even yet understand but must hereafter know, that we love one another as he loved us, calls for the entire renunciation of interest in one's self as the center of life, and the entire sacrifice of the individual life in the life of humanity. He is a Christian, though he may or may not be religious, who makes his love for man the law that is sovereign in his life; who organizes his life to save, rather than to be saved, from whatever wrong he sees devouring the life of the world. He is a Christian who makes his life an offering to human need; who gives himself to be bread and meat to feed the hunger of his brothers; who sheds his blood to be the wine of the world's life; who discerns the crises of the world, and offers hands of faith to be stretched upon the cross of a renunciation of his own happiness, that he may draw the world under the dominion of right. He is a Christian whose passion for the perfectibility of man enlarges his sympathies to appropriate the sin of the world as his own, that he may bear it away, though it mean the mortal agony of his soul in Gethsemanes of solitude. And that act, that force, that process, that society, that economy, that world, is Christian which partakes of this sacrificial and redemptive quality.

Nature is Christian.   All its forces are love forces, and its processes sacrificial.   Its ends are redemptive.   This differs from both the old theological and scientific views of nature. The theologian and the materialist, the pietist and the atheist, have shut God out of their world.   Each has had the same basis of faith in the unethical nature of nature.   Each has assumed the antagonism of virtue and nature ; of the spiritual and physical.   St. Augustine, the gnostic, follows Christ's philosophy of life no more than Mr. Spencer the materialist. Both theology and materialistic science have proceeded from the gnostic or dualistic basis of faith.   Yet evolution steadily moves toward the recognition of the fact that nature is Christian.   Evolution is the greatest redemptive thought that has come into the purely intellectual life of man.   Natural science has all along been a revealed word of God, however unconsciously it may accept or unwillingly acknowledge its true vocation.   But evolution has opened the world to God from which he

had been shut out by both theology and atheism. Through whatever doubts and despairs,
whatever perils of faith, evolution may lead,
it is yet surely leading us from the starving
and hardening transcendence and omnipotence
of the God of the theologian to the immanent
vitality and fatherhood of the God of Christ.
Whether it knows it or not, evolution is leading the physical, theological and social sciences
straight to the incarnation and the cross.
Reluctant as these sciences may be in following, deny as they may the way they take,
they are none the less being led to become
disciples in the school of Jesus, the scientist
from whom all our sciences will at last have
wisdom to learn.

Jesus constantly appealed to nature as justi-
fying his being and precedure. He was truly
scientific when he related the naturalness of
faith and moral growth to the growth of the
lily ; one life, one growth, one beauty, was in
each. Christ was infinitely more scientific
than the scientist when he appealed to the
perfect harmony of his sacrifice with the re-
productive processes of nature as instanced by
the grain of wheat. Against the view that sin

and selfishness have their seat in the flesh, in natural forces and tendencies, Jesus viewed the grossest fleshly sins as leaving man fitter for the kingdom of God than the pietism and separatism of the religionist. The only men he denounced as apparently incurable were the religiously self-interested who had dissociated themselves from their fellows, and the religiously irreproachable who crucified him for his teachings. The eighth chapter of Paul's letter to the Roman Christians is the greatest word on evolution ever spoken. He saw all the agonies and processes of nature, all the pain and travail of the earth, all the crises of history, all the experiences of man, issuing in the perfect moral development of the race, as that development is fulfilled in Jesus. The Christ is the perfect product of nature ; the perfect revelation of what nature is. The cross that came from the heart of God to redeem the world, to reveal the heart of the Son of Man, came also from the heart of nature. God and nature and the Son of Man were all working the same work. Jesus is nature's offering to man ; nature's reason for being. To those who have eyes to see, nature

teaches the lesson taught by the incarnation and
the cross. Nature, which is but the manifest
motherhood of God, in her birth pangs for the
sons of God, appeals to Jesus as her defense,
her justification, against the theologian and
the scientist ; against the pietist and the secularist ; against the deadly dualism that separates God from his world in the thought of
man ; that separates man from his brother.
The word of nature is the word of God made
flesh ; the revealed secret of nature is the
character of Jesus. The millenniums of world-
making, the ages of flood, the ages of ice, the
ages of fire, were all preparing for the Christ-
man. The forces that robe the earth with
verdure, that rib the hills with granite, that
woo the rose from the bud, that pull the oak
out of the acorn, that tear the lightnings from
the clouds, that spread the lava of Vesuvius
across the valley, that lay the coal and silver
and gold and iron in their strata, all find their
perfect interpretation, their articulate utterance, the fulfillment of their power, the disclosure of their beauty, in the Son of God.
Nature is Christian. It is the sacrifice of God
to man. To be a science of nature, to be a

truly material science, to discover and reveal
a natural economy of human relations, sociology must be Christian.

God is Christian.   Sociology cannot be
dissociated from theology.   Sociology and
theology will ultimately be one science.   Society depends upon theology.   Men will be
what they think God is.   We need a Christian theology that we may have a Christian
society.   We cannot have a Christian society
without a faith in Christ as a revelation of the
character of God.   If Christ is simply a divine
accident, if his character is a concession to
human weakness, if his revelation of God is
only partial, if the right that is in God is more
or less than the right that is in Christ, or if it
differs in quality from the right that inheres in
the nature of man, then neither sociology nor
theology have more than a speculative foundation on which to build ; neither can become a science.   Unless all there is of God
was revealed in Christ, unless the revelation
be eternal as well as historical, we worship a
God who is yet unknown, and we know not
whither our steps are tending.   Theology
must begin with Christ.   It must cease to fear

and learn to trust the revelation of God which
Christ has made. It must tolerate no doctrines which look dark in the light of the revelation of the Father in the Son of Man. It is
a fatal infidelity for the Christian to separate
the justice of God from the love of Christ in
his thinking; for the result can be nothing
else than the separation of religion from life.
He that sees the Son sees the Father: sees
what the character of the Father is: sees
what his attitude toward man is: sees what
God is like, and how he thinks and feels and
acts toward man. All the fullness of God's
life was in Christ. All that makes up the
character of the Father was in the Son.
Their unity, their harmony, their co-working,
was perfect. The mind of Christ was the
mind of God. He thought God's thoughts,
felt God's feelings, did God's works; and all
he said and did, all he taught and suffered,
witnesses that there are no contradictions in
the character of God. Christ upon the cross
is what God eternally is. Christ proved the
justice of God in the forgiveness of our sins.
He revealed the moral majesty of God when
he washed the disciples' feet. He manifested

3

the sovereignty of God in submitting to the
crucifixion. He expressed the love of God in
his wrath at the covetousness and hypocrisy
of the Pharisees and Sadducees. He showed
that the justice and mercy of God are one and
the same thing ; that justice is love at work,
and punishment for sin is mercy in action.
The fullness of the revelation of the Father in
the Son was made in the words of the beloved apostle : God is love. Our theological
dogmas must bear the light and be stated in
the terms of this revelation. When theology
begins to learn its knowledge of God from
Jesus, it will be saved for moral uses ; it will
be changed from the metaphysical to the sociological.

A Christian sociology will save the great
doctrines of theology from being lost in the
abstractions of the schools by translating them
into the actual experiences of man. It will
answer the question as to what the atonement
historically was by showing what the atonement eternally and socially is ; by project-
ing the idea of the atonement into the future
through the creation of redemptive social phenomena ; by disclosing and teaching the prin-

ciple of sacrifice as the vital force of history
and progress, of personality and fellowship.
Sociology is a science of sacrifice ; of redemption ; of atonement. The realization of
society is the realization of the atonement
through the fulfillment of the incarnation.
Society is sacrifice. It is the manifestation
of the eternal sacrifice of God, as it was
unveiled on the cross, in human relations.
Sociology will interpret the fact of propitiation by educating a societary conscience that
will compel every rational man to engage in
bearing away the sin of the world. A Christian sociology will save the doctrine of inspiration by showing that its real peril has been
in its being dogmatized and defended as a
past fact while rejected as a present fact
and condition of life. *The real problem of inspiration is not as to the manner in which holy
men of old were inspired, but whether there
are now holy men willing to be inspired and
consumed in the service of truth and justice.*
Inspiration is always the passion for righteousness in human relations, and the passion for
social righteousness is always inspiration. Inspiration is the final and natural moral atmos-

phere.   One thing that Jesus could not and would not tolerate, ' because it is the very spirit of false prophecy, was the condition of being uninspired.   Inspiration will finally organize the economic justice which law has no power to utter ;   which custom is impotent to procure.   The Patmos vision of John is the fulfillment of Christianity in the world, through sacrificial processes, in a history whose nations shall be governed through the immediate inspiration of God.

Progress is Christian.   It is the evolution and fruit of sacrifice.   The formative movements of history have been sacrificial and redemptive.   The ages witness that the justice procured through love, that the righteousness manifested in sacrifice, is not the enemy of man, the foe of civilization, as Satan and the old political economists would have us think, but the progress of man and the ground of civilization.   Covetousness and falsehood have never been profitable or wise, but are now and ever have been the waste of the earth and the woe of life.   Prosperity has not come through obedience to selfish principles, but in spite of them.   Lies and despotisms,

intrigues and expediences, self-will and social
caste, luxury and pride, never have ruled the
world, and never can. Behind the shadows
which our moral unbelief has cast upon the
glory of his providence, in spite of the self-will
which has been the tyrant and deceiver of
man, God has been working out the vital
progress of the world. The kingdoms and
the power and the glory are God's and not
the devil's. *This is a redeemed and not a lost
world.*

The sacrifice of Jesus upon the cross was
the disclosure of the divine government of the
world. It revealed that sacrifice and not self-
interest is universal law ; that selfishness does
not belong to the nature of things, but is the
anarchy of life and the negation of society.
The character of Jesus proves that the world
is grounded in right and not in wrong ; that it
has never been the dominion of evil, but has
been ruled by a righteous will in spite of its
rebellion. The world has always been the
dominion of God's almighty love, and the cross
is forever the throne of his authority and
majesty. In the midst of the throne, from
which the beloved apostle saw the glory and

authority of the universe proceeding, there was not an omnipotent despot ruling in irresponsible power, but a Lamb that had been slain, the divine almightiness manifesting itself in perfect sacrifice. The cross is the revelation of the nature of all real power and true progress as sacrificial and from within, and not arbitrary and from without. Through faith in the sacrifice of the Son of Man, God built the world, and thereupon history proceeds to its goal in a race perfected in divine sonship. The redemption accomplished by Christ was the immovable establishment of the government of God in the world. With this redemption the nations must reckon. From this standpoint the philosopher must think. In the light of this revelation the market must calculate. Upon this foundation politics must proceed. With this fact every consideration and work of man must begin. We dare not qualify Christ's authority, or amend his law of love, or consent that men shall proceed upon any other basis than the triumph of his right. Unto him has the government of the peoples been given. Unto the realization of the divine government in human

relations Jesus gave the name of the Kingdom of God. There is no other progress than
the coming of this kingdom. Progress is
henceforth the organization of redemptive
facts and the advance of redemptive forces.
Expediency is now and evermore, as it always
has been, the foolishness of history.

After the enthronement of the righteous
government of the world in the incarnation,
after its disclosure in the sacrifice of Christ, to
accept selfishness as belonging to the nature
of things, to assume that strife is the power of
progress, and that only an immediate self-interest can move men to the highest endeavor,
is to make one's self a witness to horrible and
blasphemous lies. So long as men reject the
love of Christ as the wisdom and authority
and power which God has manifested for the
guidance and government of the nations, they
cannot think with reason or act with justice.
Upon this foundation of rebellion and moral
unreason, the sacredest institutions of religion
and law and society but make systems that
must perish ; but rear structures for the dust ;
but build for the confusion of the sons of
men.

Social order is Christian.   The incarnation
of the Son of man is the revelation of the
social order in which God created and is perfecting the world.   Society is the fellowship
of the sacrifice of Christ in human relations.
The growth of the social organism is the increase of eternal life in human motives and
products, making each unrecorded thought
and forgotten deed an undying note in the
harmony of man with God and nature which
has been the song of prophecy and the surprise of science.   Society is the fulfillment of
nature in man, and the indwelling of God
with man, through the obedience of man to the
law of life enunciated by Jesus in his new commandment to love one another sacrificially
and redemptively, as he loved us.   The birth
of the social consciousness, with which the
world is now in travail, is the conversion of
social institutions from the protective to the
redemptive basis ; from the Roman to the
Christian conception of society.   The discovery of men that they may advance together
in the fulfillment of righteousness, that they
may act as one person in bearing away the sin of
the world, is the awakening of society to its

self-consciousness in the light of the universal
unity which was the vision of Jesus.

This waking consciousness is perceiving
the meaning of law in sacrifice. Law is love
speaking its mind, and sacrifice, the method
by which law achieves justice. In so far as it
is just, in so far as it is eternal, in so far as it
expresses the mind of God, law is redemptive
rather than protective. Our courts cannot
become courts of justice until they become
courts of redemption ; until they are able and
just to forgive sins, and apply the blood that
cleanses from unrighteousness. Our codes are
not lawful until they become the definition of
redemptive facts, and their execution the application of redemptive forces. Legislation
partakes of anarchism until it becomes the interpretation of the law of love, which does not
mean the omission but the administration of
punishment. The law of love is punitive because it is sacrificial, and protective because it
is redemptive. Except the law take the slain
Lamb into its heart, and ground itself in the
order that is the fellowship of sacrifice, it
cannot discern between justice and injustice.
The love of Christ is the only law that can

organize all the economies of man in a redemptive progress that shall realize the natural social order of the world in a kingdom of heaven.

The Christ-order of society reveals the simplicity of human relations. It is our self-deceit, our shrinking from implicit obedience to the law of love, our unfaith in the wisdom and power of that law, that keeps us in the fog of social doubt. It is a subtle dishonesty that cries for rules to regulate social details, rather than for principles to regenerate the social life and create a social organism. The problems of society, with all they involve, can be settled simply, orderly, wisely, and permanently by Christendom honestly accepting Jesus as the living Saviour and King of the actual life of man. Louis Kossuth, the Hungarian patriot, in recently speaking of the social revolution which he believes to be everywhere impending, said: "If the doctrines of Christianity, which are found in the New Testament, could be applied to human society, I believe the social problem could be got at." If the church would lift its eyes awhile from ecclesiastical proprieties and material values,

and cease its disputes about definitions and
metaphysics, it might see the Son of man
coming in the day of its holiest visitation, and
find itself in danger of the same attitude
toward present problems and opportunities as
that of the Jewish temple toward the divine
visitation that was its opportunity and judgment.

No other than a Christian sociology can
have a scientific ground, or produce any intel-
ligible science of society. Jesus only has revealed all the facts and forces of life. The
social order which he has disclosed is the only
basis upon which we can build with holy purpose ; with faith of soul and joy of heart ;
with a common understanding of what we are
about. *To reform society is to Christ-form it.*
By faith in Christ as a perfect revelation of
nature, a perfect revelation of God, and a perfect revelation of man, we have a sure foundation on which to build, and we know what the
building must be. The foundation will not
change, for the right in God and the right
in man are the same, and the building we
have here from God is eternal in the heavens.
His right is henceforth the foundation of prog-

ress, and his love is its law. We have only
to build upon this foundation and obey the
law of the cross, and the unity of God and
man, of heaven and earth, will be realized in
a society which shall be God manifest in the
flesh.

Through the incarnation of the eternal sacrifice and spirit and power of his love in the
man Christ Jesus, God has witnessed to the
divinity of our humanity and the humanity of
his divinity, and the unity of all life in the
heavens and upon the earth. God has not
left us to our own devices, to be tossed to and
fro upon uncertain doctrines of life, but has
revealed what our life is, what its resources
are, and given us in Christ a vision of its destiny. Our human life is not a failure, a mys-
tery, a tragedy, a crying in the dark, but a
psalm of hope, a progress along a plain path
to a divine end, an eternal rise through the
light. That which seems dark and tragic in
our life, terrible and remorseless in the processes of nature, cruel and improvident in
history, is beautiful and good, merciful and
prophetic, orderly and connected, when interpreted by faith in Christ as the destiny of

man, the evolution of struggle, the crown of nature, the meaning of history, the fulfillment of life. We know whose children we are, what our work is, what ideal of life we must realize. Though we are conceived in sin, our Father has not left us in the dust, nor taken his Holy Spirit from us, but has manifested his mightiest power in the redemption of our world. If we walk in the light as he is in the light, we shall have the fellowship of a divine society, and the blood of Jesus, his Son, will cleanse us from all sin.

The foundations of society are hid with Christ in God ; and yet they are being manifested in the glory of the larger social faith in Christ that is both restraining and purifying the almost universal passion for justice and brotherhood. There has been a wide diffusion of Christianity at the expense of its quality ; but now its life is about to be renewed and empowered. We are in the beginnings of a new redemption of the earth through the application of Christianity to life. Society is being sprinkled with the blood of Jesus. The redemptive is displacing the police conception of justice. Industry is on its way to Damascus. The Spirit of Christ is coming to anoint the factory, the mine, the railroad, to preach good tidings to the poor, and set at liberty them that are bruised. Every school of thought is feeling the pressure of a new and universal dispensation of moral energy. From Westminster Abbey to the forests of Africa, from the Roman Vatican to the mining camps of western America, men are feeling the pain and expectation of a new social order. "We have arrived," as Mazzini once said, " at one of those supreme moments in which one world is destroyed, and another is created." Though what it shall be, does not yet appear, we who know in whom we have believed are sure that the juster order, the changed world, will be like him ; that it will not be a world of fragments, of individuals, of divisions, but of members of the body of Christ.

A Christian sociology will no doubt have to defend itself against the theologian and the scientist ; against custodial religion and social egoism ; against pietist and secularist. Theology does not yet believe that God is Christian, and science does not yet see that nature is Christian. Such a faith is unknown to institutional religiousness, and can mean nothing but the complete overthrow of all social despotisms.   Such a vision is an offense to pietism, and hateful to secularism.   Between the unbelief of organized religion in the Christianity of God, and the unbelief of organized selfishness in the Christianity of nature, Christ is likely to come to a new crucifixion.   In this crucifixion, the sociology that follows Christ, will have to share.   But its resurrection will be a Messianic age, educated in the science of redemption to bear away the sins of society and bring in the thousand years of peace.

II.

THE CHRISTIAN CONSTITUTION OF

SOCIETY.

The worst enemy of the better is the good. The church needs to rise to a broader conception of its social mission; and unless the friends of the church bring about a reformation from within, we shall have a revolution forced upon us from without. The scepter of the kingdom of God will pass from the hands of the church to some institution better adapted to realize the spirit of fraternal helpfulness and mutual good will between all sorts and conditions of men, in the concrete and vital relations of industry, commerce, family, society, and state. A church united in a common devotion to the divine ideal of social service has a glorious future. A church divided into hostile and rival centers of self-edification is a dead and useless cumberer of the ground, and the ax is already at its root. With this unity of spirit, diversities of form may, and doubtless will, continue to co-exist; but when, as is too frequently the case, the form has devoured the substance, the letter has killed the spirit, and social service is lost in zeal for self-edification, then " the issue vital or fatal for the church " is close at hand.— *President Wm. Dewitt Hyde.*

THE CHRISTIAN CONSTITUTION OF SOCIETY.

The Christian constitution of society is unwritten. The most perfect expression in letters of the divine government of the world, of the unseen yet appearing just social order, is that which is known to us as the <u>Sermon on the Mount</u>. There is a true sense in which this may be called the Christian constitution of society. It is in no sense a sermon, least of all a discourse on individual piety, but a political document, given on a political occasion, as truly as the Great Charter or the Declaration of Independence. It is Jesus' most deliberate public utterance, probably the fruit of years of obedience and the toil of meditation. The multitudes had come to hear him in much the same spirit that their fathers gathered about Judas Maccabeus, or the Scots about Wallace and Bruce, or the Italian patriots about Garibaldi and Mazzini, excepting the larger meaning of the term Messiah in the Jewish mind, in which mind religion and legislation, God and politics, were inseparable. It was to a political organizer, as truly as to a religious teacher, that the people supposed themselves to be coming. His own announcement of the drawing near of the kingdom of God, following the preaching of John the Baptist, had aroused a tumult of popular expectancy. Jesus met the expectancy honestly. The Sermon on the Mount is the divine politics with which Jesus answered the inquiries of a people eager and waiting for the news and facts and forces of the kingdom of God. It is the larger legislation of God, given to the people through a greater than Moses, from a platform as vaster than Sinai as the world is vaster than Judea. It sustains the same relation to the universal society as the legislation of Moses sustained to the Jewish society. It is as truly an evolution from the constitution of the Hebrew commonwealth as the oak is an evolution from the acorn ; as the person of Jesus was an evolution from his nation. It is the most perfect piece of constitutionalizing, giving the simplest and directest ground of legislation, the world has ever received. It has its preamble, which we call the beatitudes; but they are the most revolutionary political principles ever stated. It has its laws, with retribution for disobedience all the more terrible because it is moral, and inheres in the nature of things and men. It has a conclusion, to the truth of which the progress of the world bears witness. The laws of this constitution are definite, comprehensible, rational and meant to be obeyed. It is the profoundest and plainest disclosure of the natural and eternal social order of the world that can be made in speech or letters. It asserts the only facts which can ground society in nature, and reveals the only forces which can construct it according to the social pattern of God.

Nothing so witnesses to the moral apostasy of the church, to its actual unbelief in the righteousness of Jesus, as the postponement of obedience to this constitution to some remote millennial age of magical peace. The greatest sign of the degradation of the pulpit is its gingerly treatment of the teachings of Jesus concerning right and wrong, regarding them as mystical in meaning and incompre-

hensible in application, while uttering as
eternal certainties metaphysical doctrines,
about the pagan meaning and history of which
both pulpit and pew know practically nothing.
No process of reasoning is so morally and in-
tellectually imbecile, so unworthy of the re-
spect of honest men, so subtly evasive and
cowardly, as that which conceives of the Sermon on the Mount as an unattainable ideal
handed down out of heaven for the gaze of individualistic religiousness. The Sermon on
the Mount is the utterance of the principles
that are eternally real, not only in the heavens
above, but in the ordinary relations of the
earth beneath ; not only in the far-off future,
but in the immediate present, and in all that
progress brings to the present from the past.
There is no sense in any other principles ;
neither justice nor reality.

The Sermon on the Mount is the letter, the
statute book, of the Christian constitution of
society. It is the divinest law-making that
has been done, or doubtless can be done,
for the sons of men. But it is not itself the
constitution of human relations. The constitution of society is as much more than the

Sermon on the Mount as the person of Jesus is more than his words.

The Christian constitution of society is not a church. The gathering of the peoples under the dominion of a religious institution has never been the idea of God. The purest institutional rule of the world would yet be other than a Christian rule. An institution of religion is not a constitution of society. It is at best but a medium through which the Spirit of God may pour upon society the anointing of Christ, and constitute it in the likeness of Christ. Society is not an institution, but a life. Institutions are a means to the divine social end. They are but the scaffolding of the living social temple, and shall be taken down when their work is done.

All the systems, institutions, and temples of man, in whatever age and civilization of the world, have been more or less perverse attempts to commune with God. The history of man is the drama of his futile reaching after God, through temples of stone, through institutions of religion and law, without the obedience and sacrifice of the life unto God. By the way of Babel tower and Jerusalem temple,

by the way of institutions of philosophy in
Greece and of law in Rome, by the way of
cathedrals and schools of theology in Christendom, have men sought to climb the skies of
truth, and appropriate the power of God,
without the surrender of their souls to the
soul of God. It takes men long to learn that
God dwells not in temples made with hands,
neither at Jerusalem nor Samaria, neither at
Rome nor Geneva. Religious institutions are
seldom the organization, and often the ob-
struction, of the will of God. The sadness of
history lies in the fact that progress moves in
the path of the ruins of the world's most sacred
institutions. God has wrought righteousness
into human relations through the destruction
of temples of unbelief that were supposed to
be institutions of faith. The entrenchments
of custodial religion have usually ended in being the citadels of organized falsehood, and
have made the most stubborn resistance to the
will of God manifested in the evolution of
progress.

God's warning to Protestantism is Judaism.
The meaning to Israel of the temple, which
through transformations stood so many centu-

ries, was the fellowship of man with God.
The temple was the outward expression of
the communion of the people with God, in
their personal and social and national life.
The destruction of the nation came through
the people mistaking the symbol for the substance ; the shadow for the reality ; the institution for the communion. Their apostasy,
against which prophet after prophet bore
the witness of God, lay in regarding the institution as an end in itself ; in mistaking the
organization of religion for life with God ; in
conserving the inspiration of the past in un-
changing ceremonials, and rejecting the inspiration of the present, which is the moral
health of the people. They were always wor-
shiping the God of the dead, and shutting
their eyes and ears to the God of the living.
Never had Moses been so authoritative as
when Jesus was crucified. The prophets
were never so honored as when the apostles
were persecuted. Religious institutionalism
rose up then, as it had never failed to do
before, as it has never failed to do since,
and crucified life. It would have nothing
to do with a God who went meddling with

the affairs of a living people, preferring to
rule the people according to its own rules
and ceremonies. Conceiving of the people
as made for institutions, and of institutions as
made for ruling the present with the past,
the Jews changed the laws of Moses into a
system of disobedience, and made the gar-
nished sepulchres of the slain prophets the
judgment seats whereupon unbelief passed
sentence of death upon faith. When the
Lord whom the people sought came suddenly to his temple, the religious teachers,
who did not understand institutions as but
the expression of the unity of a living people with a living God, cast him out as
a usurper and destroyer. Thus culminated
then that quality of wickedness which always passes in its day for the highest
righteousness, and which imposes its unbelief
upon itself and upon the people as the
support and defense of faith.

The anger of Jesus at the Pharisees, who
were the irreproachable religious teachers of
their day, was aroused by their persistent misrepresentation of the character of God to the
people. They had so organized religion as to

conceal the nature of God, and the nature of his righteousness and justice. The religion of the temple, which religion God himself had originally inspired and ordered, had been converted by the tyranny of its priests and stupidity of its teachers into an organized lie about God. Jesus would not, he could not, consent that the people should be deceived about their relation to God and God's attitude toward them. He did not attempt to restrain his hot anger and consuming indignation at the systematic misrepresentation of God on the part of the religious teachers. At any cost to himself he would tear away this thick veil of falsehood and unfaith from between the Father and his children. He would have men know that God was their Father and that they were God's sons, though his crucifixion be the price he must pay for teaching them that knowledge. Jesus believed in God, and he believed in the people ; he believed in the soldiers and even in the politicians ; but he did not believe in religious institutions and their teachers, because they were seeking to draw all men unto themselves instead of unto God his Father and the Father of the people.

There is an instinct in institutions, in the collective consciousness of religious authorities, though they may not recognize or be able to define that instinct, that a knowledge of the real character of God means the inspiration and lifting up of the people, and a leveling down of institutional and social thrones.   The apprehension of the fatherhood of God can have no other consummation than the perfect realization of the brotherhood of man, and the end of institutional dominion.   If the people once know God as their Father and friend, whenever they become conscious that God is Immanuel, that he is their God and they are his people, then there is no more place on the earth for tyrants and priests ; for religious, or political, or theological, or industrial despotisms.   If God is the Father of the people, then all men are equal in his love ; then he who rules his brother is a tyrant, and he who serves his brother is a king ; then the institution that would dominate the world with its opinions and customs is a wicked despotism, usurping the throne of God, and the institution that loses its structure in the progress of the world, that it may bring forth the fruit of a divine social organism, is an incarnation of God. When the people come to know the real character of God, when the collective social consciousness believes in Jesus as the revelation of what God eternally is, when God and the people get at each other in a perfect reconciliation, there will be a crushing to fragments of all religious institutionalisms; all intermeddling and intermediary agencies. And the people shall hunger no more, neither thirst any more : for the Lamb which is in the midst of the throne shall be their shepherd, and shall guide them unto fountains of waters of life, where God shall wipe away every tear from their eyes.

The church is a means to an end, and that end is the kingdom of God, which is the just social order. Like the family and the state, it is one of the triune modes of the kingdom of God. It was not sent to build itself up out of the world, but to build the world up out of itself. The idea of God is not to gather humanity into a church, and make that church the embodiment of his moral dominion over men, but to make the church the incarnation of the passion of Jesus, and send it to be lost in the life of the redeemed and perfected humanity. There is no temple in that city of God, no religious institution in that universal social order, which was the vision of the beloved apostle and seer; the fellowship of the people with God was the social order of the new earth. The work of the church is the regeneration of human society; but it is not itself that society. The mission of the church is the establishment of the Christian constitution of society; but it is not itself that constitution. The conception of the church as the supreme end in itself, as being an ark of safety instead of an organ of sacrifice, has gradually converted Christendom into an organized misrepresentation of Christ. The Christian persons, the sacrificial and redemptive lives, are more in this age than any other; they are a great multitude whom no man can number; but they are not a part of the actual church organism. They are in the church but not of it. The collective attitude of the church toward God and his world, notwithstanding the many who are waiting to be led to the Calvary of a social redemption, is percisely the attitude of the Pharisees and

Sadducees that wrought the destruction of the Jewish church and nation in the day of its visitation. As truly as Jesus would have gathered Israel into the fellowship of his sacrifice, and made it a nation of redeemers, so he would now gather the church into the fellowship of his sacrifice, and send it to be crucified for the social redemption of the world. He would save the church from the leaven of the Pharisees and Sadducees; from its unfaith in God and the people; from its mistaking respectability for virtue; from its substitution of opinion for faith. The church is called to be the Christ of God to society. And it may be that only a very small remnant will hear and obey this call.

The Christian constitution of society is the person of Jesus. It is the fulfillment of the incarnation of the Son of God in a perfected world. It is the discovery of men that they are members of one body in Christ their living head. It is society come to self-consciousness through the realization of the unity of the race in the Son of Man. The self-consciousness of society is the consciousness of men that they may move together as one man

in the bearing away of sin and the fulfillment
of righteousness ; it is the collective consciousness of men that the person of Christ is the
social constitution of the world.   Humanity
the abode of God, humanity the living temple
of the divine presence, humanity the body of
God's soul, is society Christianly constituted.
The social order of the world has its perfect
symbol in the parable of the vine and its
branches.   As the branches cannot bear fruit
except through vital union with the vine, no
more can men except through vital union with
Christ their living head ; as the branches cannot bear fruit if they become fragments, no
more can men be righteous and just as individuals.   Society again has its order symbolized in
the communion supper of the bread of our Lord's
broken body and the wine of his shed blood ;
society is the fellowship of the people in perfect sacrifice.   The Christian constitution of
society is the Lamb's book of life ; it is the
social order of the communion of the Holy
Ghost.   Christianity is the society of men in
a common obedience to the sacrificial law of
love which Christ gave as a new commandment to his disciples.   Society is the Chris-

tianity of men through the order of service symbolized in the washing of the disciples' feet on the part of the Master as illustrative of his new commandment.

These early Christian symbols are no more mystical in their meaning than magical in their effect; they are all social symbols, clearly and eternally teaching that Christianity is a society, a fellowship, a unity of men under the headship of Christ. These symbols all regard a society, a divine order of human relations in the world; in not a single instance do they regard a church which was to impose itself upon the world as an institution of religion. Christ called men to repentance not because a church was at hand which they might enter as an ark of refuge, but because the kingdom of God, a divinely just social order, was drawing near to claim the citizenship and sacrifice of men in its fulfillment. The apostolic churches were fellowships more than institutions; they were inspirations more than organizations. What we now understand by a church differs as much from anything authorized or instituted by Jesus as structures

5

of marble and granite differ from life. The influences that substituted the idea of the church for the idea of the kingdom of God and his righteousness in human relations, were Greek and Roman, and not Christian; they were impositions upon the church from without. The disciples were not sent from Olivet, and immersed in the Holy Ghost, that they might bear witness to a religious institution, but that they might testify that the Christ of God is the Saviour of men, the Redeemer of the world, and the King of the nations. The church was not sent to draw all men under its dominion, but under the dominion of the love of Christ; not sent to fill itself full of the world, but to fill the world full of Christ's quality of righteousness, which is the love of God manifested in human relations. By becoming the organ of Christ's passion and sacrifice in the world, by losing itself in the kingdom of a redeemed and perfected humanity, can the church fulfill its divine calling.

"An anarchy of good individuals" is not Christianity; nor is it society; nor is it yet a church. Christianity is the society of men in and with Christ, who is our human life divinely constituted in all its relations. We can know what our common life is only by looking into the face of Christ. He is the fulfillment and perfection of the divine life that aspires and despairs, that rises or falls, in all the children of men. He is the head and representative of our humanity under all its conditions and limitations, in all its experiences and problems. He became in all things like unto his brethren that he might reveal what the life of man is when lived in communion with God. In the faith that man is the son of God, that the world of man is founded in right, he met evil at its worst, and revealed and glorified our human nature as divine in its essence and power. We have nothing to study besides him who is both Son of Man and Son of God. All there is in God that man may know, all there is in man which may have fellowship with God, all there is of the spiritual, all there is of the natural, all there is of truth and right, love and justice, law and order, knowledge and beauty, may be seen in Christ, who is God manifest in the flesh, and man socially constituted.   The predestination of men to be conformed to the image of Christ is the heavenly vision which society must obey, that it may realize the social order of the world through a collective progress toward unity. Social justice is the jointly fitting together of men as members of the one body of Christ.

The world has never been institutionally governed. The government of the peoples has not yet appeared, yet history witnesses that inspirations and not institutions have actually ruled the world.   The great epochal and formative movements have been the marshalling of human forces under the command of great impulsions to righteousness.   Progress has been the increasing apprehension of unseen spiritual forces ; the closing together of God and the people in the communion and power of the Holy Ghost.   The bonds of this divine social order are unseen, and yet in the crises of history their strength is made manifest in the security with which the world meets the shocks of terrible and resistless judgments.   History is the progressive disclosure of the presence and fellowship of that just society which is the city of God coming down out of heaven. And the progress of man toward the fulfillment of his social destiny in Christ has never been institutional, but inspirational, sacrificial, and free. Society is not rule and letter, institution and organization, but spirit and life ; and they must be born of the Spirit who would enter the social order of the communion of the Spirit, and see the kingdom of God. The social ideals which institutions have crucified are the unseen thrones of the divine government of the world, the increase and peace of which shall have no end. Not God *and* the people, which the Italian Revolution inscribed upon its banner, but God *in* the people, is the power that is overcoming the tyrannies and slaveries, the falsehoods and hypocrisies, of the world. The Christian constitution of society is the incarnation of the Son of God. The coming social order is Immanuel, God with us.

III.

THE GOSPEL OF JESUS TO THE POOR.

" 'So be it,' replied Enjolras. 'One word more. In executing this man, I have obeyed necessity ; but necessity is a monster of the Old World, necessity's name is Fatality. Now, the law of progress is, that monsters shall disappear before the angels, and that Fatality shall vanish before Fraternity. It is a bad moment to pronounce the word Love. No matter, I do pronounce it. And I glorify it. Love, the future is thine. Death, I make use of thee, but I hate thee. Citizens, in the future there will be neither darkness nor thunderbolts ; neither ferocious ignorance, nor bloody retaliation. As there will be no more Satan, there will be no more Michael. In the future no one will kill any one else, the earth will beam with radiance, the human race will love. The day will come, citizens, when all will be concord, harmony, light, joy, and life ; it will come, and it is in order that it may come that we are about to die.' " — *Les Miserables.*

THE GOSPEL OF JESUS TO THE POOR.

THE poor to whom Jesus preached the gospel were the people. Not many mighty, not many wise, not many prudent, not many noble, not many religious, were called. This was not arbitrarily so. The few favored ones of the earth, the strong and rich, the rulers of religion and politics, were supremely interested in keeping God and the people apart, with their own authorities and dominion between. They wanted not the redemption, but the power, of the world. It was hard for the rich to enter the kingdom of God, not because God would not receive the rich, but because they could not bear the justice of the kingdom. Poverty of purse and lands and power has been largely the history of poverty in spirit. It has been mainly the poor and the oppressed, who in all ages constitute the people, that want the kingdom of God and his right to rule the earth. The very nature of the kingdom is such that only the poor in spirit, the meek and the merciful, the pure in heart and the morally hungry, can become its citizens, and participate in the kingdom's economies and politics. It is out of moral compulsion God chooses them that are poor as to the world to be rich in faith, and heirs of the kingdom which he promised to them that love him. The extremity of the peoples has always been the birth travail of a diviner economy, a juster order. The Hebrew slaves were chosen and disciplined to be the moral rulers of the earth. When King Uzziah dies, the moral glory of God is revealed to the prophet as the real power that makes progress, and not the perverted religions and political materialism that mistake the magnificence of their degradation for power and permanence. The common people hear the Christ, the religious Pharisees and political Sadducees reject and crucify. The flood-tide of Christianity which finally submerged the thrones of the old world rose, through the souls of the poor and enslaved. John Knox's reformation swept through Scotch cottages. Cromwell's victorious Puritans were impolite, strong-hearted, plain men who believed in the Bible and feared nothing but to disobey God ; men who never suspected as possible the defeat of righteousness.   Every great revolution or reform has its rise in the strength of the people whose welfare has been subordinated to that of the rich and ruling classes.   History is an ever new surprise, and prudential and conservative calculations of the future prove unreliable, because of the unseen moral resources which God treasures in the hearts of the ignorant and despised multitudes.   Just as some trying moment develops in our friends unexpected noble and beautiful qualities, so great crises in the life of a nation call into action mighty reserve forces of which the nation was ignorant.   The divine manhood and apostolic womanhood that will yet save what is good in our institutions, and be true to the freedom which our fathers achieved by making it a preparation for a Christian democracy and a righteous civilization, may come from miners' huts ; from the dug-outs and farms of our imported Scandinavian and German peasantry ; from the workshops of the poor.   We may see that what we call the perils of immigration are the providential salvation of our nation. Not by might nor by power, but by the Spirit of God in the people, has the moral and social progress of the world been evolved. In no age has God left himself without a witness to what the people may achieve when collectively caught in the sweep of a righteous movement. The kingdom of God is the kingdom of the people. God in the people is the gospel of the kingdom.

The gospel of Jesus to the poor was the good news of the kingdom of God. The kingdom of God is the gospel of Jesus to the people, yesterday, to-day, and forever. It was not the gospel of an individual escape to some other world, but the disclosure of a kingdom of God present in this world, redeeming it with the justice of love, freeing it with the freedom of truth, and perfecting it in the progress of right. It was the glad tidings that this is a redeemed and not a lost world ; and men were called to adjust their lives to this fact of a world redemption. It was the proclamation that the divine government of the world was about to reveal its presence more fully among men through their deliverance from tyrannical and slavish notions of God and practices of human life. God was drawing near the crying peoples as a deliverer from their oppressions and a righteous judge of their oppressors. God was coming as the Saviour of the world; a Shepherd of the outcast multitudes, forsaken and despised. God was revealing himself as a friend of the wronged; as an enemy of the institutional selfishness and dominion that sought the subserviency of the people to the glory and authority of the institution. The idea of God as Immanuel, as the God of the people, as the Father of the mob, as the Redeemer of the world, and not the God and protector of the few and proud and strong, not the God of institutions and exclusivists and tyrants, gave to the poor and humble and oppressed a wholly new energy of life, and a ground for exhaustless patience. It put behind history, dark and hideous as it seemed, joyless and fragmentary as the ages appeared, a comprehensible meaning and retrospect; a goal of joy unspeakable, and a moral glory unimaginable. The revelation that God was the real ruler of the world, that above and within the apparent rule of op-

pressions and priestcrafts and devils, a righteous will was working out a just order of
human relations, was in truth the good news
the peoples of all ages pray to hear and to
believe. If God is the Father of man, and
the kingdom of God is in the world, then the
multitudes that sit in darkness may see the
vision of a world redeemed from sin and injustice, and obey that vision with a faith that
shall be the victory of the justice of the kingdom. The drawing near of the kingdom of
God was the motive and call to repentance,
demanding a reorganization of life. It was
the ground of undismayed toil through baffled
effort, and perfect peace through great tribula-
tion. The kingdom of God was the gospel of
Jesus to the poor.

The gospel of the kingdom of God prepared
the way for his coming, his dwelling, the reign
of his love and the communion of his Spirit,
in the whole life of man. It meant the fulfillment of the incarnation of the Son of God in
a race, in a world society, which should be a
manifestation of God in human relations, and
which would make all work a fellowship with
God. With God in the people, and the peo-

ple in God, whoever consents to divisions and
oppressions among men, or to a system or
economy that permits such divisions and oppressions, is guilty of blasphemy. There is
no life that is not the inspiration of God, and
no work that is not a religion. He gets nearest the heart of God, he walks closest with
God, who gets nearest the heart of the people ; who goes into the thick of human work,
and down underneath human burdens ; who
appropriates the shame and waste of the people's sins as his own, and bears them as his
sacred sorrow to his own Calvary of service.
He who would interpret God, and know what
God's work is, will not find him away from
the common toils and places of men, but in
the midst of the people, healing them with his
sympathy, building them up in unity and
Christliness with the inspiration of his presence. The people are the true tabernacle,
which the Lord pitched, not man. Jesus did
not find God in the temple, among the religious
teachers, among the men estimated best by
the institutions of religion ; for they cast him
out and would have none of his kingship or
kingdom. Where there is need and sin, where

there is work and sacrifice, there God is to be found.   God is in the hard pressure of duties bravely borne and done, in the distractions and uncertainties of life honestly met.   Where there is the sense of helpless weakness, the nerveless failing of the heart, the conscious-ness of inadequacy to do one's work, there God is to be met in the communion of human need.

Religion is not something besides life, not a withdrawal of life from fellowships, but the pouring out of life as a sacrifice to God in the service of man.   There is no falser con-ception of religion than that which speaks of the works of the world as hindrances to spiritual growth; as vocations secular and profane.   The drudgery of the world is wor-ship; it is communion and creation with God.   I am excited to more reverence when I stand in the factory than before the ca-thedral.   I have more sense of the presence of God in the midst of the work of the world, being done by the hands and minds of men, than I have in those institutions which stand wholly for the development of religious culture.   The mill, the mine, the

palace of bargain and exchange, are methods and sacraments of life with God; they
are ways in which men may manifest themselves as sons of God; they are sanctuaries
of the divinely human fellowship where God
and men may work together in the making
of the kingdom.

The immediate mission of Christianity is
the interpretation of all life and work in
the light of the kingdom of God. It cannot too swiftly tear away the last vestige
of everything that is simply ecclesiastical;
overcome every division and opinion, every
pride of tradition and polity, that breaks up
the unity of life; rend asunder all veils
that hide the presence of God in the midst
of the people and their work. The lesson
taught Elijah is still to be learned: not se-
clusion, but the obedience of life to service,
is the temple wherein God's voice may be
clearest heard. The fact that the novel is
becoming more than the preacher the social
teacher, lies in its dealing more with the
common things and common experiences of
life, and less in the imaginary romances of
kings and their courts. The kingdom of God

6

is the kingdom of the people and their work.

The gospel of Jesus to the poor is the divine sonship of the people. In an age which mammon rules, when the most selfish motives are made the ground of political appeal, when the mercantile spirit dominates society and the church, when property is protected at the expense of humanity, when the state regards material things as more sacred than human beings, the gospel of the kingdom of God, the gospel of God in the people, the gospel of the divine sonship of man, needs to be terribly preached as the judgment of love to the brutal cynicism of the market ; to the industrial despotisms that would be absolute over the work and life of the people ; to the materialism that degrades politics to a mere organization of ignorance and cunning. To seek dominion over man for the profit of material interests, or to gratify the covetousness of political conspiracies, or to establish the authority of a religious institution, is to usurp the throne of God. The most fearful blasphemy against God is selfishness with men who are weaker than ourselves. Commercial tyranny and

social caste are a war against God, and with
the blood of the Lamb, because they are a
degradation of the sons of God whom Jesus
redeemed, causing them to fall into ignorance
and despair, crime and want. Men are equal
in the love of God. No soul is of less worth
to God than another soul. God will no more
have distinctions and divisions preventing the
humblest life from developing all its divine
potentialities than he would have Satan's
throne in the heavens. No son of man is
wronged, or crushed, or despised, or kept poor
and ignorant by a social system, without God
being profaned. The unworthiest man in the
social estimation of materialistic distinctions
may be a revelation of all there is of God.
Imperial character asserts itself in the com-
monest walks of life. The poorest man who
works for his bread may wear the crown of a
divine kingship. There are men who will be
kings if you put them in pig pens, and men
who will be pigs if you put them in palaces,
and adorn them with all the artificialities of a
material civilization and the refined ignorances
of modern culture. The most unenlightenable
ignorance is generally to be found in the

schools that stand for the highest culture, and the most brutishness of human life in the centers of material refinement and acquired manners.

The kingdom of God is among the people. It is enthroned upon the moral ideals of our common humanity. The extension of its reign is the waking consciousness of divine sonship and social unity which is stirring the world to a new creation of itself. If the apostles and prophets are to be trusted, God has always been suspicious of palaces and great markets. God never gets along well with halls of philosophy and centers of art. The living literatures and arts have rarely come from the schools, but have been the overflow of the freshness and wealth of the natural life. God believes in nature, where he lives, and in the natural man, where he loves, even when man is blinded and bound by passions. God has been able to move even the fiercest natural passions under the power of great moral inspirations; but little has he been able to do with institutions which have become organs of conservatism. The Son of

Man realized the unity of the heart of nature and the heart of man and the heart of God when he walked the ripening fields and flowering hills with his Galilean disciples, whose minds had not been crystallized by artificial civilization ; whose affections had not been petrified by customs and fictions. It was childlike simplicity, open-minded, wondering and unartificialized human nature, which the moral authority of Jesus led into the kingdom of God. What we call civilization is infinitely short of the goal of progress. It bruises the divine life in man, even when you have said all you can in civilization's behalf. Polished manners, systematic theologies, fashionable clothes, the sciences of the universities, electric street cars, towering temples of trade, are not life ; in fact they are not civilization. They shame the natural faith of the divine soul of man, and repress more than educate his natural instincts to nobleness. They obscure our vision of God and his world, fastening our faith to things rather than righteousness; to values stamped on paper and anarchies of commercial architecture. God will keep bringing man's civilizations to naught till we have a civilization that is the order of his providence ; a civilization as natural as the lily, as beneficent as the wheat field. And when civilization finds the heart of nature, it will find the heart of God ; and thorns and thistles shall no more abound ; and the lion and the child, the wolf and the kid, the mistress and the servant, the rich and the not rich, shall dwell together in peace in the righteousness of the kingdom of God, which kingdom is Immanuel, God in the people.

The revelation of divine sonship is the foundation of human brotherhood under the vision of God's fatherhood. The gospel of the kingdom is the good news of the social nature of salvation. The brother sons of God are not fragments, not individuals, each working out his own redemption and perfection alone. There is a large sense in which souls *are* saved in bundles, notwithstanding Emerson's epigram to the contrary. The logical evolution of individualistic religion is atheism in practice. While each man is judged according to his work, there is also a judgment of races and economies and nations. The Biblical idea of righteousness is largely social and national. Nations and races are sent as apostles of peace and messengers of justice. Israel is God's servant and so is Persia, as truly as David and Cyrus. Christ's conception of redemption was communistic and racial as well as personal ; it was a conception of world redemption of and through society. Pentecost was the baptism of the collective consciousness of a moral community of men. The Spirit of God has always been seeking the immersion of men collectively ; seeking to realize the social order of the communion of the Holy Ghost, which is the agreement and collective impassioning of men in the pursuit of righteousness ; seeking to gather men in one accord and move them as one man in the moral conquest of the world. No man liveth or dieth unto himself ; no man is saved or lost unto himself : men are brother sons of God. All that divides man from man, that destroys his social consciousness, that gives one a sense of superiority to others, whether it be intellect or clothes, creeds or culture, wealth or social caste, is a profanation of God ; it is devilism, which is dualism.

Sin is the individualizing of one's life, the
withdrawal from fellowship with one's brothers, as truly as rebellion against God. The
organization of one's life with self as the
center is all there is of sin, whether the
manifestation of sin be sensualism or religiousness, prodigality or prosperity. Every human
life is interlocked with the destiny of every
other life, past, present, and to come. The
apostolic writer of the Epistle to the Hebrews
profoundly anticipated the fact which is the
dawning vision of science and sociology, when
he hinted that Abraham and Moses, with the
prophets gone and glorified, could not without us be made perfect. In the last analysis
of salvation, no man is wholly saved, and
God himself is not wholly saved from the
consequences of human sin, until all men are
saved in that society of universal fellowship
through sacrifice, which John symbolizes in
that sitting down together at the supper of
the slain Lamb. The race, not the individual,
is the unit. The universe is one, and it is
Christian. The incarnation of the Son of
God was the revelation of all there is in the
heavenlies, so Paul says, in our most straitened

human conditions, revealing the unity of our
life and the eternal sonship of man, which
is the gospel of Jesus to the poor.

This gospel appealed to the divine manhood
of the people. It was the revelation to the
poor of their moral dignity as sons of God. It
was the message of the philanthropy of God ;
and God does not patronize men. It was the
appeal of the strength of God to the strength
of man ; God fosters no religious pauperism.
The gospel was God's good news to men that
they could be men ; men of moral glory, men
of truth and freedom, men of divine stature,
men with an eternal life, men who could work
with God ; they could be sons of man because
they were sons of God. The philanthropy of
God, the gospel of Christ, was justice to the
people, judgment to their oppressors and de-
ceivers, and the divine government of the
world. It was the anointing of men as kings
and priests of God, as moral conquerors of the
nations. It was never the attitude of what
men understand as benevolence, the comfortable pity of the strong for the weak, but was
the call of the Father in heaven to his sons on
earth. The gospel of Jesus to the poor was

the appeal of the humanity of God to the divinity of man ; the appeal of the deeps of God to the deeps of man ; the appeal of the moral glory of God to the moral glory of man ; the appeal of the freedom of God to the spirit of freedom in man ; the appeal of the love of God to the justice of man, and of the justice of God to the love of man. The saving power of the gospel was its revelation to man of himself ; its good news to the poor of their citizenship and kingship, their freedom and reign, in the kingdom of God, the kingdom of the heavens and the earth.

The gospel of Jesus to the poor was the democracy of the people. Pure democracy and pure theocracy are one. Democracy is the communion of the people in the social order of the Holy Ghost ; and theocracy is the government of the people by the immediate inspiration of God. The democracy of the people has not yet been manifested ; but our social troubles are preparing the way for its realization ; and when it appears in social justice, it will be the incarnation of him who first preached the gospel of democracy to the people.

Our industrial society has had brought down to it all the conflicting and the uniting elements of past stages of society. The forces at war in modern society are not new, but old. The principles that fight for supremacy in our industrial society are the same that fought in the subjection of provinces to oriental monarchs; in the long strifes between the popes and the nations; in peasant wars and insurrections; in the Puritan, French, and American revolutions of the people against the divine right of kings. The principle of absolutism, and the principle of democracy which we have long thought triumphant, are here in the social problem, drawing up their longest and strongest and most fearful lines of battle at our doors. The doctrine of the divine right of the king to rule the people, of the divine right of the pope to have upon his shoulder the government of all peoples, has been translated into the doctrine of the divine right of property to govern the social well-being of the people for its own gain. The people may not be able to define what they know, but they know that they are serving and toiling with hands and brains for masters who are absolutely irresponsible for their welfare, and absolutely authoritative in the government of economic production and distribution, of employment and unemployment. The social question is simply the field upon which the forces of democracy and absolutism are deliberately and knowingly preparing for their greatest conflict. Whether the conflict be moral or military depends upon whether the church receives or rejects the social incarnation and redemption of the Christ who preached the gospel that has been responsible for all the revolutions, however much their violence misrepresents him, since he gave to men the vision and motive of the kingdom of heaven upon the earth.

The social problem is the problem of democracy against absolutism; of the people against irresponsible masters; of freedom against the institutional dominion that would subject the living present to the dead past. It is not a problem of wealth and wages merely, but of the right to work; the right to do one's duty; the right to sacrifice; the right to live as becomes a son of God; the right to be free.

People will starve and die; they will live in dug-outs and tenements and miners' huts; *but they will be free.* And the freedom wherewith the kingdom of God shall make them free is the freedom of the Son of God.

We sometimes hear it said that young men and women of to-day have no incentive to heroic action, such as inspired the heroism of the great epochal days that have made men free in the past. But I say to you that there were no opportunities in the constructions and reformations of the past that opened such doors of service and sacrifice, of moral glory and pure courage, as now open to you in the coming of that social redemption of the world, which is but the uprising of the sons of God in the preparation of the way for the coming of his kingdom.

The old passion for freedom comes to us vaster and regenerated; it comes to us with universal and heavenly meaning. It is not now freedom for Switzerland, freedom for France, freedom for Puritan England, freedom for America, that inspires the world with a quickened life, but the freedom of man. With the vision of the universal democracy of

the sons of God, Jesus has forever lighted all
the heavens of political freedom and religious
truth ; of social justice and human destiny.
The collective obedience of a thousand men
to that vision would be the creation of a new
world ; a world in which all absolutisms, be
they social or political, industrial or theological, would be overcome.

The opinion of priest and theologian, of industrial master and party manager, that the
people cannot be trusted, is a denial of the
good news of the kingdom of God, which was
the gospel of Jesus to the poor.   Unbelief in
the divine sonship of man is the ground of the
practical atheism toward God, the separation
of religion from life, for which theology is
responsible.   The political leaders and the
clergy are almost unconscious of the collective
moral faith of the people because they do not
know God as Immanuel, which knowledge is
the gospel of the kingdom of God, and the
ground of all democracy ; of all faith and freedom.   It was the faith of Moses and Jesus, of
Milton and Mulford, of Mazzini and Lincoln,
that the people are abler than any institution
to organically express the will of God in a

communion of justice. The living faith of the living people in the living God is defeated and inarticulate because they have no organ through which they can express their faith.

But there draws near the kingdom of God which shall organize the faith of the people in a democracy of justice, in a social order of the Holy Ghost. And our call to repentance toward God as Immanuel, and to faith in the people as sons of God, is the good news of the coming of God's kingdom among men, which was the gospel of Jesus to the poor.

IV.

THE MESSAGE OF JESUS TO MEN OF WEALTH.

" Progress is the consciousness of progress. Man must attain it step by step, by the sweat of his brow. The transformation of the *medium* in which he lives only takes place in proportion as he merits it ; and he can only merit by struggle ; by devoting himself and purifying himself by good works and holy sorrow. He must not be taught to enjoy, but rather to suffer for others ; to combat for the salvation of the world. It must not be said to him, *Enjoy ; life is the right to happiness ;* but rather, *Work ; life is a duty, do good without thinking of the consequences to yourself.* He must not be taught, *To each according to his wants*, or *To each according to his passions*, but rather, *To each according to his love.* To invent formulæ and organizations, and neglect the internal man, is to desire to substitute the frame for the picture. Say to men, *Come, suffer ; you will hunger and thirst ; you will, perhaps, be deceived, be betrayed, cursed ; but you have a great duty to accomplish ;* they will be deaf, perhaps, for a long time, to the severe voice of virtue ; but on the day that they do come to you, they will come as heroes, and will be invincible."— *Joseph Mazzini.*

THE MESSAGE OF JESUS TO MEN OF WEALTH.

I AM appointed to present to you, this evening, what I understand to be the message of Jesus to men of wealth, and to apply that message to the problems of society which the best thought and truest sympathy of our times are reaching out to solve. I assume, in what I shall say, that I am addressing an audience of Christ's disciples.

In their essence, the social problems of today are not different from those of yesterday; they are as old as society itself. They date back to the infancy of the race, when sin couched at the door of Adam's eldest son, to spring up within his heart as hatred for his younger brother. Ever since Cain — whom President Hitchcock calls "that first godless political economist" — killed his brother Abel, the associability of human beings for good and common ends has been a problem; a problem, be it kept in mind, born in a heart of covetousness, and set by the hand of hate for the race to solve. Cain's murder of his brother Abel was the first bald, brutal assertion of self-interest as the law of human life — an assertion always potential with murder ; an assertion whose acceptance involves the triumph of the brute man over the God-imaged man ; an assertion which the divine heart of humanity has always denied ; a theory of society which will be remembered as a frightful dream of the past when the race recovers its moral sanity. Cain's hands were the first to grasp and wield competition as the weapon of progress ; a weapon from which no economic theorists have ever been able to wash the blood of human suffering. When Cain replied to God, "Am I my brother's keeper?" he stated the question to which all past and present problems of man's earthly existence are reducible. The search for the final and comprehensive answer to Cain's question has been the race's sacred sorrow ; and obedience to such an answer would carry in it the perfect solvent of all the problems that perplex the minds and hearts of men.

History and prophecy have always pointed toward a time of industrial peace and social brotherhood. The most unselfish aspirations of the noblest men have been along the line of the social unity of the race. About this hope statesmen and philosophers have woven their sublimest theories of society and government. It has been the highest inspiration of poetry. It is the end toward which Moses and Plato looked. It is the lofty strain borne along from prophet to prophet through Israel's glory and shame. Outside of Biblical prophecy there is no purer expression of this ancient hope than in John Stuart Mill's autobiography : "I yet looked forward," he says, "to a time . . . . when the division of the produce of labor, instead of depending, as in so great a degree it now does, on the accident of birth, will be made by an acknowledged principle of justice ; and when it will no longer be, or be thought to be, impossible for human beings to exert themselves strenuously in procuring benefits which are not to be exclusively their own, but to be shared by society to which they belong."

And yet, with all the history and prophecy,

the schools and temples, the philosophy and poetry, the governments and civilizations, the day of brotherhood seems no nearer than generations ago.   The hope grows faint with age. The problems of society are still unsolved.

The question of Cain is the master question of our age.   It has grown articulate with the greed and cruelty of history.   It threatens our American day and nation with the crisis of the centuries.   It must be answered ; and answered with justice and righteousness.   The blood of Abel cries out through toiling millions.   The expectation of the poor shall not forever perish in hopeless toiling and longing for better days.   As John Ruskin says, "There are voices of battle and famine through all the earth, which must be heard some day, whoever keeps silence."   No arrogant reply as to the historic and legal rights of private and corporate property will silence these voices.

The natural development of our civilization will not unfold the solution of our industrial problems.   When we watch the mammoth enginery of this modern civilization through the assurances of a partisan press, or the mer-

cenary declamation of the politician who esti-
mates the moral stupidity of the people by his
own, the movements of its great wheels seem
wonderfully safe and perfect ; but when we,
in our sober, honest, thoughtful moments,
view it through the sympathies and purposes
of the divine Man of Sorrows, we see torn,
bleeding, mangled, sorrowing, famishing multitudes beneath the wheels of its remorseless
enginery ; we see that greed and not love is
the power that moves our civilization ; we see
politics, commerce, and the social club moving on the economic assumption that selfishness is the only considerable social force, and
assuming that civilization can advance only
through the equal balancing of warring, selfish interests ; we see men valuing brute cunning and the low instinct of shrewdness more
than whiteness of soul.

A civilization based on self-interest, and se-
curing itself through competition, has no power
within itself to secure justice. We speak to
pitiless forces when we appeal to its processes
to right the wrongs and inequalities of society.
The world is not to be saved by civilization.
It is civilization that needs saving. A civili-

zation basing itself upon self-interest has a more dangerous foundation than dynamite. It is built upon falsehood. It carries in it the elements of anarchy because it has no ground in moral realities. It is atheistic because it treats God and his righteousness as external to itself. It is nihilistic because it thrives on destruction. It is a civilization which Bishop Huntington declares "leads by a sure course to barbarism." It is a civilization under whose procession John Stuart Mill affirms the very idea of "justice, or any proportionality between success and merit, or between success and exertion," to be "so chimerical as to be relegated to the region of romance." The end to which the civilization of the present tends is material, and not moral ; it tends to the enslavement of society and the smothering of its highest life. Civilization is the flower of the character of the dominant classes ; it is an effect more than a cause ; its forces originate in character ; its activities are the expression of the people's being. No civilization can be made righteous, or can make itself righteous, by any restraints or regulations external to itself. A righteous civilization can have no other source than the inward righteousness of those who originate and control its forces.

There is no power in abstract truth, either economic, ethical, or theological, to cure our social ills. Economic laws have dealt with things external to man's being; with prominence apart from inward forces of character. Ethical truth taught to an un-spiritualized race, or generation, or civil-ization, is a childish waste of time and strength. There is no ethics apart from religion. The springs of human virtue are all in God. There is no ethical truth other than the expression of the will of God. Socrates, Plato, and Shakespeare seem to have understood this better than some of us who teach our fellow-men to-day. Nearly all the warnings of the Old and the New Testament, which we so self-assuringly address to so-called unbelievers, were addressed in the first place to those who presumed them-selves to be already in the kingdom of God ; to those in the temple services and the churches. The ethical instructions of Jesus and the apostles were all based upon, and

developed from, the cross. Theological truth
has repeatedly shown its barrenness of the
fruit of righteousness. The darkest crimes
of history have been committed by the
conservators of religion. A jealousy for
theological truth often accompanies a hatred
of duty. The Pharisees were so orthodox
that they crucified Christ for heresy. They
possessed the oracles of God. Yet the
truth did not save them from greedy,
heartless, malignant, hypocritical lives. A
slavish and enslaving conservatism has
always joined hands with an indifferent
worldlyism for the crucifixion of God's per-
ennial revelations of incarnate truth. I sus-
pect the devil knows more truth than any
of us ; and he is all the more devilish for
knowing it. Truth that does not strike its
roots in love is a curse ; and the truer the
truth the more accursed its results. There
is a pregnant thought, which the church
has yet to learn, in a saying of Mozoomdar's
in his "Oriental Christ:" "Unless our creeds
fertilize the world, and our lives furnish meat
and drink to mankind, the curse uttered on
barrenness will descend on us."

We cannot look to the state to solve our social woes and grant our social hopes. All the great political prophets, from Moses to Milton, and from Milton to Sumner and Mulford, recognize that the people are the makers of the state rather than the state the makers of the people. The state is the expression of the highest common thought of the people ; it is the work of the people's faith. Hegel says that " the state is the realization of the moral idea" of the people. The people must be righteous before the state can be righteous. If we agree with Milton that the state " ought to be but as one huge Christian personage, one mighty growth or stature of an honest man," then the Christian state must be the offspring of a Christian people. If we regard the state, with Sumner, as a grand moral institution, it must be moral because the people build it with their moral thought and purpose. The best and strongest institutions have been powerless to restrain people whose moral conceptions they did not embody. The Mosaic legislation was never fully enforced. Roman law could find no expression in the thought and life of later Rome. Alfred the Great

incorporated the Ten Commandments and the
Golden Rule in the early English constitution,
but they are yet far from being the laws of
English industrial and social life.   Laws written on tables of stone and printed in statute
books are but the playthings of politicians if
they are not written in people's hearts.   Laws
cannot make men unselfish. They can restrain ; but all legal righteousness is but tem-
porary.   Police righteousness is not divine
righteousness.   Force-justice is unreal justice.
The state cannot, by any possible process,
make the rich man unselfish, or the poor man
thrifty.   The state cannot establish justice
and righteousness on the earth ; but justice
and righteousness must establish the state.
Except the state be born again, it cannot see
the kingdom of God.

   The heart of all our social disputes is what
Mulford calls " the crude assertion of an en-
lightened self-interest as a law of human
activity."   This assertion is the essence of the
gospel which Professor Sumner proclaims
from his chair in a great Christian university.
Social classes, he decides, owe each other
nothing ; benevolence is simply barter, and

"the yearning after equality the offspring of
envy and covetousness." This is a gospel
which would have caused the proclaimer to be
mobbed in the streets of Athens in the days of
Pericles ; a gospel which would have astounded
Moses, and seemed ancient and barbarous to
Abraham. The supremacy of the law of self-
interest is the conclusion of Herbert Spencer's
materialistic philosophy ; and of the wretched
pessimism of Hartmann and Schopenhauer. It
is the principle upon which Cain slew his brother.
It was the seductive whisper of the serpent
in Eve's ear. It is the principle upon which
crime is committed. It is the principle upon
which the capitalist acts when he treats labor
as no more than a commodity subject to the
lowest market rate and the law of supply and
demand. It is the principle upon which railroads are bonded and bankrupted for private
ends. It is the law by which the New England deacon chattels his money upon the
Dakota farmer's meager possessions at a
usurious and impoverishing rate of interest —
a deed which will not be obscured from the
eyes of a just God by the endowment of a
chair in a denominational college. It is the

principle upon which a Chicago financier proceeds, with no more moral justification than the highwayman's robbery of an express train, to "corner" the pork market, and thus force from the hungry mouths of toiling families a million and a half of dollars into his private treasury — a deed for which the giving of some thousands to found city missions and institutions will be no atonement in the reckoning of the God who judges the world in righteousness and not by the ethics of the stock exchange. The law of self-interest is the eternal falsehood which mothers all social and private woes ; for sin is pure individualism — the assertion of self against God and humanity.

God's answer to Cain's question, God's solvent of the social problems of our day, is the cross. And the cross is more than an historic event. It is the law by which God acts, and expects men to act. It is the creed of God which will never be revised. It is the principle upon which creation and history proceed. It was the assertion intensified which God has been making through all history, of self-sacrifice as the law of human development and achievement. Self-sacrifice is the law which God asserts in Christ over against the law of self-interest which Satan asserts in Cain. The trial in progress is Christ *versus* Cain. The decision to which the times are hastening us is, Shall Christ or Cain reign in our American civilization ? And well may the heavens await our decision in silent and awful wonder ; for we are deciding the destiny of the earth !

The message of Jesus to every man, rich or poor, weak or strong, ignorant or wise, is the cross. In whatsoever form he puts it, whether in parable or principle, miracle or command, the cross is the heart of every message : not *a* cross, but *his* cross — the cross of absolute self-renunciation which he carried in his heart. In Christ's teachings the cross was something else than an arbitrary contrivance for populating heaven. The gospel of our Lord knows of no reconciliation *by* the cross that does not begin with a reconciliation *to* the cross. Being reconciled to God has a vaster meaning than being reconciled to the comfortable reception of certain benefits from God's hand. It means the apprehension of

the law of God's life as the law of our lives.
And sacrifice is the law of the life of God.
The creation involved an infinite sacrifice.
Out of the travail of God humanity was born.
Before earth's sinning, sorrowing ages began,
with infinite sorrow God consented within
himself to their beginning. The sorrow of
Gethsemane was in God's heart before he
breathed life into man ; and the suffering of
the cross continues in the Father-heart till sin
vanishes from the hearts of his children.

The moral progress of the race has been
through sacrifice. It is the divine order of
culture. The race's divinest types are always dying that the race may live. The
world has thriven on the sufferings of those
who have loved it and given themselves for
it. Every new truth which men have learned
has been read in the blaze of martyr fires.
Every great reform has been won at un-
reckonable cost. A Calvary is the tribute
Freedom always claims from men. Every
commercial privilege which an American
enjoys was purchased on Golgotha. We
are not our own ; and that which we have
is not ours. Every breath of our bodies

and every opportunity of our hands, hearts, and brains was bought for us with immeasurable sacrifice. Our little lives are surcharged with the blood-bought wealth of the centuries ; and not one of us, if we could live to the age of Methuselah, and held in our grasp the wealth of the continents, could begin to pay the future the debt we owe the past. Sacrifice is not life's accident, but life's law. No man has a moral right to live other than a sacrificial life in this world of sin and sacrifice. Lotze affirms that no life is moral which is not self-sacrificed in the service of others. No Christian is true to his Christ, nor has grasped the meaning of the cross, who is not a vicarious sufferer for his fellow-men. The cross was not our release from, but our obligation to, sacrifice. And whenever there is a heart throbbing with the passion of Jesus, there will be a life straitened till its mission be accomplished. Wherever there is a soul pulsing with the life of God, there will always be sacrificial hands uplifting humanity to higher things.

Now, the reason this message of the cross

8

has so much larger an application to men of wealth is that they have the larger opportunities and possessions to sacrifice. They have the weapons of love. Christ offers no different terms of discipleship to any American man of wealth than he offered to Matthew at his custom-table. The centuries have not bulged the needle's eye. It is as hard to enter now as when Christ mentioned its smallness to the rich Pharisees. Christ was infinitely pitiful to the weak, the poor, the thriftless, the sinful, the ignorant ; but to those who sought to hallow covetousness with religious forms, and convert piety into a cloak for greed, he had but wrath and scorn and scourges.

The simple fact of our industrial situation is that the men of wealth in our American churches can begin to solve our pressing social problems any time they choose, by simply being disciples of the Lord Christ. As the Father sent Christ into the world to sacrifice himself in the service of man, so Christ sends the corporation manager, the merchant, the mill owner, the mine operator, the street-railway president, to be a living sacrifice in the

service of men. Christ was under no more
obligation to consecrate himself wholly to the
world-saving, man-uplifting business than every
business man in America. The uniqueness
of Christ's work has no bearing upon this fact.
The claim of God to Christ's service is the
claim that rests upon us all. The Lord did
not die to give us an opportunity for self-
seeking. We are not here on a vacation
from God. He sends forth every man of
wealth to be a saviour of his fellow-men ;
and the business man who fails to be a
Christ to the world has made a disastrous and
irreparable business failure. A man of business has no more right to make personal
profit the supreme purpose of his store, his
shop, his capital, his factory, his railway,
than Jesus had to work miracles for personal
profit. We have no more moral right than
our Lord to direct our social, domestic, or
financial affairs for personal ends. The
Christian has no more right to an unconsecrated horse, or house, or dress, than Christ
to an unconsecrated cross. We are not our
own ; we are bought with a price ; and
nothing short of an unreserved surrender of

of self-interest to God's interest in humanity is moral or just. Not to be self-sacrificing in others' service is injustice. To be unloving, even to the unlovable, is to be ungodly.

The day is coming when the homes, the shops, the stores, the social clubs, the newspapers, the corporations, the political caucuses, that have not for their sacred purpose the making of men divine will be regarded as out of place in a world that has been redeemed by the Son of God and nourished by the life-blood of his saints. There is no such thing as a secular affair in the universe of God. There is nothing but moral anarchy outside of the realm of God's authority. God recognizes nothing as having a right to exist apart from a vital relation to himself. There is no affair which engages human passions, brains, hearts, hands, that is not a religious matter. Nothing has a moral right to an existence on the earth which has any other basic purpose than the uplifting and sustaining of men in righteousness. The basing of commerce, or education, or politics, or society, on the modern atheistic and mercantile idea of secularity is an assumption that violates the lesson of history, and is intolerable to the Scriptures. Christ is King! Unto him every knee shall bow. The freedom of the race is to be reached only through yielding to Christ's moral despotism. As President Valentine has said, "There is nothing under the stars that is not amenable to his authority." There are no exemptions provided for stock exchanges, or wholesale establishments, or railway corporations, or social leaders, or politicians, or teachers of natural sciences. Whatsoever ye do, in word or deed, do all in the name of the Lord Jesus. We have no moral right to dress simply with a view to pleasing ourselves; eat as we please; live in the kind of homes we please; ride in the carriages we please; have the company we please; buy the books, pictures, jewelry, luxuries we please — no more than Christ had.

I am aware that what I am saying is irritating to this practical, untheocratic age — an age which has small sense of the divineness of things. We have little practical use for things we cannot buy or sell; things that do not minister to our bodily comfort and social pride. We are apt to measure even the religious value of men by their market value. We are willing enough that Christ should have been crucified for us, but are angered at the thought of being crucified for him. It is so much easier to worship Christ than go up and share with him his cross. It is so much easier to be obsequious in saying Lord, Lord, than it is to do the things he tells us ; so much easier to subscribe to creeds and repeat rituals than renounce selfish ownership to one's possessions and deny one's self. But only a crucified Christianity will ever be able to win a selfish world to the crucified Christ. And there is no other name under heaven given among men whereby society and civilization can be saved. Not until the race shall have been crucified with Christ's crucifixion will it assemble with clasped hands and free spirits around the throne of the Lamb.

Men first quarreled with God, and they have been quarreling with each other ever since. And the reconciliation of men to each other must proceed through their reconciliation to God as he is revealed in Christ. Social unity must be the result of God-one-ness and God-in-ness. It will be the

outgrowth of the incarnation of the divine
sacrificial Christ-life in the life of humanity.
When men touch each other with the touch
of God, and love each other with the love of
God, and serve each other with the sacrificial
heart of God, then the race will be one con-
cordant family. The solvent of every problem of society is the love of God. And the
cross is the weapon which God took from his
own heart to break open our hearts that he
might pour therein the life-renewing balm of
his love. Our hope for social freedom will
reach its fulfillment, not through social mech-
anisms, but through our acting, as Frederick
Maurice says, "in the faith that the constrain-
ing love of Christ is the mightiest power in
the universe." Society is to be saved by men
and women who shall pour their lives and
possessions as streams of love and service
into the great current of Christ's redeeming
life, whose onflowing is healing the nations.

The whole question of labor and capital,
and all the problems of our day, can be re-
stated in this form : Is the Gospel of Jesus
livable ? God is calling to-day for able men
who are willing to be financially crucified in

order to establish the world's market on a Golden Rule basis. He is calling for noble women who are willing to be socially crucified to make society the agency for uplifting instead of crushing the poor and ignorant and weak. "Whoever," says Benjamin Franklin, "introduces into the public affairs the principles of primitive Christianity will change the face of the world." It is for this work that God would anoint you, O Christian business men of America! History has never presented to man an opportunity richer than yours. You can make the market as sacred as the church. You can make the whirl of industrial wheels like the joyous music of worship. You can be the knights of the noblest chivalry the world has ever seen ; not going forth "to recover the tomb of a buried god," as Ruskin said of the crusaders of Richard Lionheart, but to fulfill the commands of the eternal Christ. And where you go, flowers of hope will spring in your footprints. You can bear the weak in your arms, and set the captives of poverty free. You can cause the deserts of human despair to blossom with gladness of fulfilled prophecy, and hush the

voices of discontent in the sweetness of fruitful toil. You can give work to the wageless ;
teach the thriftless and ignorant ; seat the
poor in the best pews of your churches. You
need not strive nor cry, nor wear plumes and
flaunt banners ; but you can be the heralds of
a new civilization, the creators of a Christian
industry whose peaceful procession will reach
around the globe. You need carry no crosses
of wood or gold or silver ; but you can bury
the cross of your Christ deep within your
hearts and stretch forth consecrated hands to
realize the life of humanity by upraising it into
the idealism of Jesus. You can draw the
world's trades and traffics within the onsweep
of Christ's redemptive purpose. You can
plant everlasting peace underneath the feet of
men, so that there shall be no more strife ;
and light earth's night of toil with skies of
love, so that there shall be no more night.
You can be the makers of the new earth
wherein dwelleth righteousness ; in which the
race will be at last human because it is divine,
and divine because it is human.

God's new day of judgment is surely and
swiftly dawning. Voices from out the future

are crying repentance unto this mammon-worshiping generation. The ax is laid at the root of the trees. New John Baptists are arising who will speak truth and justice to the Herods of finance, though their ecclesiastical heads be the price of the message.

In the lead of human progress I see the matchless figure of the Son of God—

"Toiling up new Calvaries ever with the cross that turns not back."

Behold the Lamb of God that beareth away the sin of the world! Let us close about him, O brother men, and keep step with the march of the cross

"Till upon earth's grateful sod
Rests the city of our God!"

V.

THE POLITICAL ECONOMY OF THE

LORD'S PRAYER.

Our Father who art in heaven,
Hallowed be thy name.
Thy kingdom come.
Thy will be done, as in heaven, so on earth.
Give us this day our daily bread.
And forgive us our debts, as we also have forgiven
our debtors.
And bring us not into temptation, but deliver us
from the evil one.

THE POLITICAL ECONOMY OF THE LORD'S PRAYER.

POLITICAL economy, when it becomes a science, will teach society how to so regulate production and distribution as to provide for the economic needs of all. Economic science is thus an ethical science ; it is a science of righteousness ; it is a science of the communism of justice. Whatever system fails to secure to each man the fruits of his labor, whatever science proceeds upon the assumption that it is natural and just for some workers to have more and others less than their needs, is not political economy.

The first element in political economy is prayer. The economies of man can be regulated only by the inspiration of God. Prayer is the breathing in of God's breath, the taking in of God's life, so that we may have moral and physical health to do God's will in our human relations. Prayer is more than asking for what we want; it is finding out what God wants; it is fellowship, friendship, association with God. Through prayer men and God come together on terms of mutual understanding and co-operation. Prayer is spiritual communism; it is the democracy of life. If God be our Father and we his children, if God has a will which man may know, then God is able justly to regulate the economic life of man, and associate men in perfect harmony.

In teaching the disciples how to pray, in uttering what we know as the Lord's prayer, Jesus did not mean that we should always repeat his words, but that we should apprehend the moral quality of prayer.

This prayer is vitally related to the associated life of man. It has in it no element of individualism. It is without egoism. It is a social prayer. God is not addressed as *my* Father, but *our* Father. We are not bidden to ask for *my* daily bread, but *our* daily bread. We are not to pray that *my* debts be forgiven, but *our* debts ; still further is the social obligation recognized in this petition : forgive us our debts *as we* have *forgiven our debtors;* forgive our wrongs against thee as we forgive those who

have wronged us, our undone duties toward
thee as we forgive those who have not done
their duties toward us. The disciples were
not taught to pray for individual deliverance
from evil, but social deliverance. No man
can utter this prayer, with any sense of its
meaning, without losing thought of himself in
the great consciousness of the divine and de-
pendent childhood of man. To utter this
prayer, in any sympathy with its spirit, is to
clasp hands with all the children of men as
brothers, and stand with them as common sin-
ners and suppliants before the throne of mercy
and grace. To enter the holy place of this
prayer is to meet God in a great democracy
of human need, and to lose sight of self in the
splendor and providence of God's all-loving,
all-just, and all-pitying Fatherhood.

But before any needs are named, before
bread is asked for or sins confessed to be forgiven, there must be a longing for the coming
of God's kingdom — the term which Jesus
uses to define social right and peace, social
truth and justice among men. For what is
God's kingdom but a perfect and progressive
society ? What does God will but the realiza-

tion of his love in human relationships ? The
passion of prayer, as the passion of work,
must be the oneness of men with God. It
must be the passion for what Mazzini calls
"the collective perfectionment" of the race.

Our Father which art in heaven. This is a
confession of the brotherhood of men. It
means the equality of men in the love of God,
and the right of each to do his duty in the development of all the potentialities of his
nature. It is the most revolutionary expres
sion ever uttered, and the seed of mighty
revolutions now on their way. *Our* Father
means that railway manager and brakeman,
employer and employe, rich and poor, ignorant and wise, privileged and unprivileged, are
brothers. The drunkard in the street is the
brother of the saint. The wild-hearted woman
of sin in her chamber of shame is the sister of
the clergyman, and her shame is his shame.
The vice and misery of the sweat-shop are the
ignominy of the philanthropic millionaire ; for,
whether he would have it so or not, his millions are red with the blood of the sweater's
victims. *Our* Father, means that the divisions
between human beings made by clothes and

creeds, money and culture, position and pos-
session, are but thin disguises that hide from
us the eternal childhood of the soul. *Our*
Father, leaves no refuge for caste, but makes
all separatisms, all withdrawal of man from
fellowships, all enthronement of individual
rights and privileges above the rights and
privileges of others, fearful blasphemies. Who
dares to say, *Our* Father, and then select his
neighbors, draw lines between rich and poor,
cultured and uncultured, and treat himself as
if money or knowledge entitled him to more
consideration than his brothers?

Our Father, means a democracy in the production and distribution of wealth. To shut
out mutualism, to shut out brotherhood, from
a railway office, or a factory, or a legislative
hall, or a court of adjustment and penalty, or
a social room, or a religious institution, is to
shut out the love and deny the reign of God.
The plutocracy which has enthroned itself as
lord of industrial America not only gives, as
De Tocqueville says, "the worst masters the
world has ever seen," but rejects the fatherhood of God and denies the divine government of the world; it grounds society in

9

practical atheism, and realizes both the tyranny of egoism and the anarchy of selfishness.

Hallowed be thy name. The name of God has been made known, and his character revealed, in humanity. God has spoken his estimate of the worth of man by himself becoming man. There is a sense in which what God is depends upon what man is. To dishonor man, to treat the meanest man as apart from God, is profanity. We hallow God's name by making our life a word of God ; our work with men a communion with God. To deal with men simply upon a basis of profit and loss, to forget the sacramental nature of bargain and exchange, is to profane God. He who prays, Hallowed be thy name, and then does not honor God with his ballot, with his buying and selling, is a hypocrite. He who deals selfishly with a child of God is guilty of a profanity more vicious and dreadful than the habitual oaths of the ruffian. He profanes God's holy name who says that the Sermon on the Mount has nothing to do with politics ; that the Christ quality of righteousness is not praticable in industry and society. To hallow God's name a man must live, as the old German mystics used to say, as though he himself were God. "The man shall set a watch over himself and all that belongeth to him within and without, and shall so direct, govern, and guard his heart, as far as in him lieth, that neither will nor desire, love nor longing, opinion nor thought, shall spring up in his thought, or have any abiding place in him, save such as are meet for God and would beseem him well, if God himself were made man. And whenever he becometh aware of any thought or intent rising up within him that doth not belong to God and were not meet for him, he must resist it and root it out as thoroughly and as speedily as he may." All of which is sound economic science and political wisdom. *A man must act economically, politically, socially, as if he were God, or he is a foolish and profane man.*

We hallow God's name by honoring every work of man. All work is divine; all work is fellowship with God; all work is a participation in the eternally creative life of God. Any society which regards one kind of work as less honorable than another disgraces God's name, and disowns his fatherhood. What we

call rising in the world is a social falsehood.
It is no more honorable to be a senator, an
artist, or a preacher, a banker or a railway
president, than it is to be a coal-heaver or a
brakeman. There is no such thing as rising
in the world by leaving one occupation for
another. All such distinctions are the social
fictions we inherit from a pagan social philosophy. The gospel of the crucified Working-
man, the coming of his kingdom of God, is
the redemption of all life and work from the
superstitions and tyrannies of false sciences of
society. Sawing wood is as honorable as the
pursuit of philosophy. All disinctions between the degrees of honor that should be
accorded to trades and callings, to quantities
of wealth and social castes, must be swept
away before there can be peace and mutualism, redemptive law and just order ; before
there can be a wise economic science, or a
human society that shall hallow God's name.
Often, what men call rising in the world is a
falling from a divine into a material state.
He rises to the sublimest height who finds the
work which he can do best to serve men, be
it shoveling coal or legislating for the state, or

directing the work of his fellowmen. If a man can serve his Father and his brothers best by making bricks, or mining coal, his work is as honorable, is as truly a hallowing of God's name, as the preaching of the gospel, and his work is to be treated as sacredly as the divine right of kings was treated. All legislation which privileges one class above another, which protects property more than persons, which exalts wealth above work, dishonors God and violates the prayer which asks, Hallowed be thy name. A true political economy will be the science of such a diffusion of the products and benefits of civilization that there shall be no gradations of honor in the works of the world, and society shall be a Christian commune of art, literature, science, philosophy, and religion.

Thy kingdom come. The idea of a kingdom of God, of a world in which men would be under the direct rule of God, and the nations governed by the immediate inspiration of God, is the dream of history. This divine government of the world, this realization of the social order of heaven among men, is the hope that neither prophet, nor warrior, nor ruler, nor priest, nor poet, nor the great heart of the people, would ever wholly yield. Cyrus and Cromwell, Isaiah and Mazzini, were led by a vision of a kingdom of universal righteousness, however crude were sometimes their notions of right. The Hebrew nation was born into this conception of the kingdom of God. The Revelation of John closes with the majestic vision of the earth redeemed unto universal brotherhood, united in one fellowship of sacrifice, the tabernacle of God spread over it, and the word of God written in the faith and read in the obedience of every heart. *The interpretation of history is the coming of the kingdom of God.*

The gospel which the apostles believed and preached was the good news of the presence of the kingdom among men. The advent of Christ was the drawing near of that kingdom with forces to deliver men from their sins ; from their tyrannies and slaveries. Unto Christ had the government of the peoples been given, with all authority in heaven to redeem and all power on earth to save, until the kingdom should be delivered complete unto the Father. The apostles went forth to claim the world, with all its governments and economies, its religions and relations, as Christ's ; unto him was every affair of man amenable. No blasphemy would have seemed to them so terrible as the partitioning of life into the secular and the sacred, the economic and the spiritual ; as the division of any part of life from the sphere of Christ's authority. *The gospel of the kingdom was the glad tidings that this is a redeemed and not a lost world;* that men could live here upon the earth, amidst the hardest human conditions and most desperate circumstances, lives of divine sonship through faith in the Son of Man. The gospel was the glorious command that men should organize their lives under the dominion of the law of love which ruled the life of Jesus ; the law of love that was interpreted by the sacrifice of the cross ; the law of love which is the judgment court of the kingdom of God.

The church has failed to fulfill the kingdom of God in a society of just relations because it has not believed in the political or economic practicability of the law of love. It has been guilty of a vast profanation of God in dividing human life into the secular and the religious.

Secularism is atheism reduced to practice. The theory that the whole actual life of the world must be lived out under the dominion of self-ishness is the science of treason to the kingdom of God. No theory of conversion, no saving of souls from the world for the church, no philosophy of the atonement and the future life, can take the place of the gospel of the advent and triumph of the divine society. The apostolic conversion was a turning from self-interest to sacrifice as the law of life. The repentance preached by John was a purification from social wrongs as a preparation for citizenship in the kingdom of God. The salvation of Jesus was a redemption from covetousness and pride; from selfishness and social caste; from false systems and oppressive customs; from all divisions among men and rebellions against God.

The kingdom of God is the dominion of the law of love in the whole life of man, with all its activities and processes.

It is a political kingdom, offering the freedom of God to its citizens. We have a conception of political freedom as the right to

pursue one's own happiness ; of moral freedom
as the right to choose between good and evil.
But the right to achieve happiness is not
political freedom ; nor the right to choose
between good and evil moral freedom.   Freedom is subjection to the right ; it is obedience
to the will of God.   Freedom is deliverance
from the sphere of self-interest, from the
misery of self-concern, from the tyranny of self-
will, from the slavery of the pursuit of happiness, through the mastery of truth and the
service of citizenship in the kingdom of God.
The freedom wherewith Christ makes us free
is the deliverance from self through the sacrifice of love for our brothers.   The realization
of the freedom of man is the fulfillment of the
kingdom of God in a society of perfect justice.
The achievement of the true freedom is the
acceptance of the divine government of the
world proclaimed in the gospel and revealed
in the cross of Jesus.

The kingdom of God is a political economy.
It is the good housekeeping and divine thrift
of the state.   It is the regulation of production and distribution through communion with

God.   It is economic justice through the fellowship of sacrifice.   It is a natural law which
commands us to seek first the kingdom of God
and his righteousness.   The kingdom does
not come to destroy but to fulfill prosperity.
If God is good, if truth is true, if right is wise,
if love is law, then it must be natural that
obedience will bring the largest progress and
best civilization.   If God is not able to man-
age the affairs of state, if his laws are not
practicable in society, if they are not a wise
economy of industry, then God and man and
nature are a unity of failure.   Since there is a
kingdom of God, since that kingdom has
overcome the world in the Son of Man, the
constitution of that kingdom can be the only
political economy.   All gain through selfish
ways is everlasting waste, and only the righteousness of the kingdom is eternally profitable.
Every man who loses something for Christ's
right's sake enriches the life of the humanity
of which he is a part.   And Jesus says clearly
and often that he who is not willing to make
an offering of his life for the sin of the world,
who will not deny self-rulership and bear the
cross of self-renunciation, is not worthy to be

his disciple, and cannot be a citizen of the kingdom of God.

The kingdom is coming in the world, whether we and our age want it or not, and we must reckon with its coming. If we receive the kingdom, it may come without observation ; but if we resent its coming, it will grind us to powder in the fury of revolutions.

To pray, Thy kingdom come, in spirit and in truth, is to pledge our powers to the preparation of the way of that kingdom in our home and city ; in our economies and politics ; in our life and in the world. Our work with God for the fulfillment of his right, will be our glory in the victory of faith that shall make the nations of the world the kingdom of God, under the authority of his Christ.

Thy will be done, as in heaven, so in earth. Wherever God's will is done, there is heaven ; for heaven is harmony. A man rises, he ascends into heaven, he is spiritualized, he is glorified, the more perfectly he comes in accord with the will of God. And wherever self-will asserts itself against God's will, there is hell ; for hell is discord, anarchy. We descend into hell, we harden ourselves for torment and the flames, we separate ourselves from fellowship with God and men, by passing under the dominion of self-will.

That God has a will concerning the earth and all things therein is the testimony of all prophecy and the word of all history. To say that there is anything that cannot be immediately directed by the will of God, that there is anything without the sphere of God's interest and government, is atheism, though we call it secularism. There is no work in which man engages, nothing which his thoughts cherish or energies pursue, that is not under the pressure of the will of God. His will of love pursues every man and institution ; every activity and organization. God has a will concerning the management of railways ; concerning municipal politics and police ; concerning national finances ; concerning the inmost domestic details ; concerning the social systems and political economies of men. Otherwise God would not be our Father ; he would not be almighty and all-present, all-wise and all-good. And all that keeps the earth from being heaven, is the self-will of man which refuses to know and do the will of God.

We have no other work than to do God's will. Our occupations are the channels through which that will flows in the enrichment and enlargement of the life of the world. Our works are the ways that God has put into our hands to execute his will in human relations. Unbelief in the possibility of knowing and the practicability of doing the will of heaven upon the earth has been the sin of all our economies.

I do not deny that a basis of faith, which is simply obedience to one's moral reason, is essential to a knowledge of God's will. We cannot know the will of God through listening to what our moral philosophies and mercantile sentiments call the dictates of conscience. There is no surer way for the world to reach perdition than the very broad way of conscientiousness. It is true that there is a voice that speaks in the deeps of every man's being, calling him to a higher life. But it does not follow that what a man does is right, or that it is the will of God, because his conscience seems to him clear. Conscience is a safe guide only when God is the guide of the conscience. Conscience will compel us to righteousness when conscience is educated in righteousness. The despotisms and inquisitions, the crucifixions and commercial frauds, the false economies and social castes, have been supported with some measure of conscientiousness. The most incurable wickedness in the world, the wickedness of self-will and religiousness, generally finds its way through the world in the light of a clear conscience.

He that willeth to do God's will as it is revealed in Christ, as it is revealed in love and sacrificial service, has a ground of faith from which his moral reason may apprehend the whole will of God, in its moral quality. Not until we make our life an offering to the divine will, to be sacrificed in the supply of human need, are we in a position to know that will. Only the life that is a living sacrifice can know the will of the Father in heaven, and do that will, as it was revealed in the cross of Christ. No man knows what is right or wrong, except he learns it for the interest of some one besides himself. None discern between truth and falsehood save such as read the truth in the white light of a passion for righteousness. Except a man take the slain Lamb into his heart, he cannot discern between justice and injustice. Through the renunciation of self, which is the beginning of all wisdom as it is of achievement, we both learn and execute God's will. He whose interest is absorbed in himself, who views the world as the sphere of self-acquirement and self-enjoyment, may live what to the world is an exemplary life of integrity, what to the church is a life of eminent Christian usefulness, but yet a life which may be an antagonism to the will of God. Only he whose thought and interest, whose purposes and energies, are absorbed in fellowships of service, whose life grows through sacrificing itself in other lives, is that moral attitude toward God, and has that quality of sympathy with God and man, that alone can interpret the will of God. None but such as see in the world the opportunity for self-offering can know the will of God concerning the management of railways ; concerning bargain and exchange ; concerning the governments and economies of society ; concerning the management of mills, factories, mines, wages, and profits. He that willeth to do the will of the Father of our Lord Jesus Christ shall know that will.   And that man only is honest in praying, Thy will be done, who makes his prayer an offering of his life to be sacrificed in doing the will of God on earth as it is done in heaven.

Give us this day our daily bread.   A truthful and intelligent utterance of this petition is the taking upon one's self of a vast social obligation.   This prayer for daily bread is a voluntary participation, on the part of him who truly prays it, in the fatherliness, responsibility and providence of God.   It means that we who thus pray must be intent upon making society the organ of God's providence ; that we dare not be indifferent to a social system which defeats a divine economy of production and distribution ; that we must, like Jesus who taught us these words, be terribly discontented, hotly indignant, and wrathful, at the inequality of burdens and benefits which a false science of society permits.   Our right to gain and enjoy is an idle matter compared to our responsibility to reveal God to men as their Father.   For any of us to claim what we have as our own, to make gain the lord of our energies while voices of hunger and murmuring fill the world, to be indifferent to wrong social conditions, to consent that millions shall have only poverty for their portion and the few control the wealth of the world, and then pray for *our* daily bread, is to be guilty of a horrible hypocrisy. Society, to be just, must be the organ of the providence of God to the people. When we consent to an unproviding social system, to a political science that is not a science of providence, we witness to men that God is not their Father ; we make way for tyrannies, and raise fearful unbeliefs between men and their freedom.

The investment and distribution of wealth, which economists have spent so much wisdom in showing to be according to natural and economic law, has been arbitrary and unnatural, revealing economic foolishness and producing economic disaster. We have been taught that wealth responds to the greatest demand ; that it invests where it can find its greatest security and interest. But wealth has done precisely the reverse of this. It has utterly failed to meet the natural demands of God and men, and has scarcely ever failed to prove its cowardice and greed, and witness to

10

the falseness of its theory, by fleeing from
every just demand.   Wealth is losing itself
through saving itself.   Its withdrawal from
circulation and productive investment in times
of panic, its habit of hiding itself in vaults
and refusing to work and sacrifice in the face
of a crisis, is disobedience to both ethical and
natural law ; it is uneconomic and suicidal.   A
sound business sense, a natural economy of
investment and distribution, would bid capital
go where it is needed ; where it can supply the
demand for work and wages ; where it can be
the manifestation of the providence of God to
his children.   In this way capital would obey
the true science of supply and demand, and
find its enduring prosperity.   Capital can
prove its right to be only by being as inven-
tive and ingenious in providing for the prosperity of society as for its own increase.
Unless individual wealth soon faces and ac-
cepts its social opportunity and responsibility,
it will go the way of political and ecclesiastical absolutism.   In seeking the good of society, in seeking first the justice of the Kingdom of God, in seeking the Christ-order of
society, wealth would obey a true economy,

a scientific economy, and in the end have all things added to it by natural processes. By answering the prayer, Give us this day our daily bread, will wealth prove itself to have a natural and divine right to social protection. There has not been a single financial panic in recent American years that could not have been averted, and converted into a divine opportunity for a sound progress, by the response of the capital in Christian hands to the immediate social need. Wealth is always a social production and responsibility, viewed economically. Viewed ethically, a crisis and time of unemployment and want, a time of social extremity, is the supreme obligation and opportunity of wealth to at least furnish work and bread for the society whose protection has made wealth possible. The tenement house system, the system of monopolies, the system of land aggregation, the sweating system, the system of municipal public works, the railway system, the whole industrial system, the present crisis, is the divine, and perhaps the last, opportunity of the collective Christian capital of America to lay in peace the foundations for a Christian society. This collective Christian

capital is under the same quality of an obligation that God is to answer the prayer, Give us
this day our daily bread.   It is under as great
an obligation to build factories, and open new
fields of industry, because of compassion on
the multitudes as Jesus was to spend a healing
sympathy on the sinful and the sick.   Let the
ingenuity of wealth become social, let its energies be naturally and divinely directed, let its
forces become redemptive, let its ends be the
social well-being, its concern the common
health and wealth of the people, and it will
have discovered a true economy ; and it will
create a new world. Jesus was under no more
obligation to give his life for the world than is
the collective Christian capital of to-day to
give its money for society in the creation of
a Christian democracy of industry.   Except
wealth become the manifestation of the providence of God, except its economy be an
answer to the people's prayer for daily bread,
except it so administer itself that in seeing it
we see the fatherhood of God, except it believe on the Lord Jesus Christ, it cannot be
saved.   Mystical as this may seem to a so-
called practical business world, it is both sci-

entific and rational. And if there is any sphere of life among men where there is a lack and need of sense it is in the practical business world of to-day.

Forgive us our debts, as we also have forgiven our debtors. It is hard to speak of the forgiveness of sins as a social obligation, and keep out of the way of the theologian, who insists on separation and distinction between forgiveness and atonement, between propitiation and justice. Such distinctions are metaphysical and artificial; they belong not to morals or philosophy. We must be rid of all metaphysical and legal definitions of forgiveness and punishment, propitiation and redemption, before we can think of the sociality of the forgiveness of sin. Forgiveness is not passive, not sentimental; nor is it a bargain between God and man; nor is it yet definable in the terms of the court room. But one who forgives is always one who expiates the sin he forgives. Forgiveness is, after facing the enormity of another's sin, voluntarily taking that sin upon one's self, that the guilty one may be delivered from its power. The forgiveness of sins involves the most strenuous moral activity.

It is the very energy of virtue seeking to bear away sin not its own. We do not forgive by letting the sin against us pass into pleasant unremembrance, by letting by-gones be by-gones, but by appropriating the sin we forgive as our own, and expiating, burning it up, in the holy flame of our own suffering on behalf of the forgiven one. Forgiveness and salvation are the same. When the sin of the world is so real to us that it makes life a divine agony, when the injustices and littlenesses and shame and failures of our brothers become so real as to hurt, to crush, to make us bleed upon the cross of self-renunciation, and make the righting of the wrong of the world the passion of our life, then the forgiveness of sin becomes a real experience, a moral fact, a working force in our life ; then we become expiators, sin-bearers, atoners, propitiations. Nothing less than the whole life at work delivering from sin is forgiveness. To forgive our debtors is to pay their debts. This voluntarily going down underneath the sin and wrong of the world to bear its misunderstanding and mockery, to be mangled and tortured by it, to bear it through Gethsemane to

Calvary, is the divinest of all mysteries; the simplest and holiest of all facts; the most evolutionary of all processes; the most social of all economies. It was in this way that God forgave our sins in the incarnation, and revealed the cost of that forgiveness on the cross. The forgiveness of sins is the foregoing of sins.

The artificial and metaphysical theories of forgiveness have prevented the coming of that Christian society which is a fellowship of forgiveness and salvation through sacrifice. Jesus organized a redemptive society, not a church or religion or sect, to be the organ of his forgiveness and passion to the world. He did not himself come to bear away the world from its sin, but to bear away sin from the world, and perfect its social order through moral fellowship with man. This divine society was to execute his forgiveness; to incarnate his propitiation; to disclose his government and realize his atonement in human experience. He left no room for mistake concerning the work of this Christian society. There is nothing ambiguous about his definition of the quality of life that entitled men to citizenship in the kingdom of God. His society was to be a fellowship of those who should bear his cross of suffering for the sin of the world; a society of men and women as distinctly dedicated to sacrifice as the slain Lamb himself. The whole idea of a church, which was to be an ark of safety from the world, is absolutely foreign to the conception of Jesus. Many were called to become citizens of this kingdom, members of this society, then as now, and few were chosen. Many could be good Jews, good pagans, irreproachable in manner, correct in opinion, very religious; but few were great enough to become members of a society of organized sacrifice. And this organized sacrifice was not for personal ends, for saving the souls of its members, but for executing the forgiveness and working out the redemption of Christ in a perfected world.

Society must learn how to forgive sins. Our courts must become able and just to forgive and purify. It is the state's business to forgive sins as truly as it is the business of God. The state must be the social organ, and society the living organism, to discover

how to apply the redemptive forgiveness of
Jesus to persons and administer it through
institutions.

The forgiveness of sins is a rational law of
political economy. The administration of
this law in the case of the Homestead strike
might have made it the Pentecost of an industrial dispensation of the Holy Ghost. The
economic waste, the countless millions that
are yearly lost, through the economic viola-
tion of the law of forgiveness, witness to the
financial imbecility, and how much more to
the ethical wickedness, of an economy that is
not the justice of love.

*And bring us not into temptation, but de-
liver us from evil.* An intelligent utterance
of this petition proceeds from a faith in the
government of the world by a righteous and
overcoming will. It is grounded upon a faith
that God's goodness is at work, even in the
darkness and disorder, fulfilling ·righteousness
in the world. To make this prayer is to offer
one's life in the service of the world's deliverance and need. In this way we put into
God's hands the forces which he uses to get
his will done. By our unity with God's will,

by centering all the forces and wishes of our life in getting done his will, we ourselves become living incarnations of that will, so that men may see our works to be the works of God, and glorify our Father in heaven ; so that men may see what God wants by seeing what we want ; so that God may make us living Bibles, in which our fellow-men may read his will ; so that our lives may be manifestations of God's thought ; so that we may be words of God made flesh.

The pathos of history is the cry which goes up from every age for God to lay bare his holy arm, and right the wrong that is in the world. It seems to each age as if the will of God were slow in getting itself done.   But the slowness is more seeming than real.   And our offering of ourselves as sacrifices for the world's deliverance, our prayers and agonies for the judgment of the world in righteousness, are the accumulation of the moral forces that shall at last prevail in a regenerated society, a new earth. They are the accumulation of the spiritual forces for the world's purification which John symbolized in the golden censer of the prayers of the saints.   The moral intensity, the Holy

Ghost power, the passion for righteousness, of one age is carried on to, and increased by, the next, until we have what we call revolution. The prayers of the saints are poured out upon the earth; and there are thunderings, and lightnings, and earthquakes; there are retributions, and judgments, and redemptions; there is a Protestant Reformation, a French Revolution, a Puritan Commonwealth, and an American Civil War. God will deliver the world from evil, and bring it out of temptation, at any cost to the world, at any cost to himself. To utter a prayer for the world's deliverance from evil, without any sense of its meaning, without any expectation of fulfillment, without the intention of making our life a brave and holy protest against the evil, without offering ourselves as sacrifices in behalf of the world's deliverance, is to be guilty of a terrible hypocrisy, and to fearfully condemn our own souls.

We must remember, too, in praying, in offering our life, that evil is political, social, economic, ecclesiastical; that it is manifested in human relations; that it is with social relations that the gospel of Jesus mainly concerns itself. We need to recognize that we live in an economic age, which, with all its progress, differs from the middle ages in the fact that the feudal barons acknowledged the responsibility of furnishing work and bread for the people, while the industrial lord acknowledges no such obligation. We should pray with the knowledge that the widening and deepening gulf between the rich and poor, between the church and the world, is an evil that means dreadful judgment ; an economy that is the science of foolishness, an anarchy that means the destruction of our institutions, unless we make our lives prayers for the deliverance of the people of God.

The divinity of Jesus life was his perfect faith that God's will can be done in the world, his doubtless purpose that God's will shall be done, and his whole offering of himself in the service of that will, to deliver the world from evil and bring it out of temptation. By this spirit that made Jesus believing and resolute and sacrificial must we be led as sons of God, for whom the world of social travail and sorrow now waits.

Men sometimes ask why God does not himself remove the evil of the world, since all

power and all love are his. The reason is
that God cannot. Deliverance from moral
evil cannot be other than a moral process —
the voluntary response of will to will. The
will of God in the world is not like the will
of the engineer over the locomotive. In a
moral universe there can be no such thing
as an arbitrary will. God might strike the
evil things in the world by lightnings of destruction, and the world be no better for the
method. Only as man wills what God wills
can the world be delivered from evil. God's
power to deliver man is limited, because of
the very nature of that which is moral, to
man's willingness to be delivered. To compel
a man to do right acts does not make a
righteous man. God can remove evil only
by processes that make men eternally alive ;
that make men love right and hate wrong.
Correct conduct may accompany a wholly
hardened and self-centered will. Only as we
love God's will, and rejoice in it as a will that
can be everywhere known and done, can his
will deliver us from evil.

But I think that God is asking why we do
not deliver the world from its evil. God is
crying unto men, out of the depth of his

father-heart, where the cross eternally is, to be delivered from the shame, the heart-ache, and the punishment of the evil that is devour- the life of his children. *God is praying to men to deliver him from the evil of the world.* God is asking why we, with the almightiness of his love, with the all-power of his sacrifice as our resources, with the Son of Man as our conqueror and king, do not rise up against the evil of the world as one man, rise up against it in the Messianic power of a societary self-con- sciousness, and bear it away, that it may no more make miserable slaves and god- less tyrants in the world. *Deliverance from evil is God's prayer to man as truly as man's prayer to God.* When we answer the prayer of God, then our own prayer will already be answered, and the authority of Christ will have prevailed over the nations.